FINDING MY VOICE

ALSO BY THIS AUTHOR

Novels
A Reasonable Lady
A Sky for Arcadia
An Unreasonable Daughter
Virgin Hall

Short Story Collections
CityScapes
Wakonta Calendar

Poetry
Breaking the Surface

FINDING MY VOICE

a personal history of the Silent Generation

JANET TALIAFERRO

BOLD STORY PRESS
CHEVY CHASE, MARYLAND

Bold Story Press, Chevy Chase, MD 20815
www.boldstorypress.com

Copyright © 2026 by Janet Taliaferro

All rights reserved. No part of this book may be reproduced or used in any manner without written permission of the copyright owner except for the use of quotations in a book review. Requests for permission or further information should be submitted through info@boldstorypress.com.

First edition: 2026
Library of Congress Control Number: 2025917186
ISBN: 978-1-954805-95-8 (paperback)
ISBN: 978-1-954805-96-5 (e-book)

Cover photo courtesy of the author
Cover and interior design by KP Books

Printed in the United States of America
10   9   8   7   6   5   4   3   2   1

To the millions of volunteers who make our political system and government operate.

CONTENTS

Preface ... ix
CHAPTER 1 Awakening in the Great Depression ... 1
CHAPTER 2 What I Learned at My Mother's Knee ... 7
CHAPTER 3 Roots ... 17
CHAPTER 4 War ... 27
CHAPTER 5 The Duration ... 35
CHAPTER 6 School Days ... 51
CHAPTER 7 University ... 63
CHAPTER 8 Married Life ... 75
CHAPTER 9 Passing the Torch ... 87
CHAPTER 10 Dallas ... 95
CHAPTER 11 My Days in Court ... 101
CHAPTER 12 Learning the Trade ... 107
CHAPTER 13 Virginia ... 123
CHAPTER 14 The House in McLean ... 133
CHAPTER 15 The Business of Campaigns ... 147
CHAPTER 16 Addiction and Recovery ... 163
CHAPTER 17 Another Sharp Turn ... 173
CHAPTER 18 Settling In ... 179
CHAPTER 19 One Last Trip Around the Block ... 191
CHAPTER 20 Facing Reality ... 197
CHAPTER 21 On My Own ... 205
CHAPTER 22 Looking Toward a New Century ... 213
CHAPTER 23 Returning and Writing ... 225
CHAPTER 24 Annus Horribilis ... 241
CHAPTER 25 A Final Decision ... 247
Epilogue ... 251
Acknowledgments ... 253
About the Author ... 255
About Bold Story Press ... 257

PREFACE

THE DECISION TO publish this book was made on a sunny June morning in 2024. I was standing at the window of a hotel in South Bend, Indiana, facing the classic county building. In front of it stands a column topped with the figure of a young Union soldier. In his left hand he clutches a battle flag while his right hand points south and his head is turned slightly as if to urge his imaginary comrades into battle. The figure, in full battle dress, is young and fit. I think of a recently removed statue of another young man, dressed in the army uniform of the enemy the Indiana lad had wished to defeat. That second statue was called "Appomattox." The lithe figure stands with his head bowed and his hat tucked under his crossed arms. The dejection of defeat is obvious in every line of his body.

Appomattox no longer stands in the center of Washington Street in Alexandria, Virginia; it was removed along with some arrogant equestrian statues. Apparently, no one noticed the difference between the message of defeat signified by Appomattox and the victorious stance of a mounted Robert E. Lee. I mourn the loss of the figure that depicts the acceptance of defeat.

Sixty-eight years and twenty days divide the end of America's Civil War and my birth date. Now, at ninety-two, my life has spanned a time when the country was never more united to a time when it is nearly as divided as it had been during those crucial nineteenth-century years.

I am part of the silent generation born between 1925 and 1945. The name was given to us by *Time* magazine in 1951, the same year I entered university. We were given the name because we were considered conformists. There is validity in the charge of conformity; we were rule followers. As children born during the Great Depression many of us were old enough to remember World War II, and we tended to do things exactly as our older brothers and cousins of the "Greatest Generation" did. We learned to be rule followers because, like those older family members, in war you follow orders or die. However, the impression of docility or disengagement ignores the reality that our generation fought its own war in Korea and staged the first lunch-counter sit-ins when the civil rights movement began. It was our generation who welcomed Black students in graduate schools all around the country and participated fully in the civil-rights and women's movements. Most importantly, we went to the moon. In a way our generation was less silent than ignored. The World War II veterans were busy building lives. Those younger than us were busy making noise.

Also, we were leaderless. The leaders of our generation—the Kennedys and Dr. King—were assassinated too young to lead us into a new millennium. The politicians born in the 1930s did not last long in office, except for Walter Mondale and Birch Bayh. The political atmosphere of wartime cooperation began to bifurcate into liberal and conservative. The World War II generation would occupy the White House from 1948 until George Herbert Walker Bush left in 1992. Jimmy Carter, a southern progressive, could be considered one of us as he continued to be an activist. Certainly, Robert F. Kennedy, born in 1925, and Dr. Martin Luther King, though born in 1929, spoke to and for us.

I began writing this memoir in 2000 as an informal account of my life for my children and grandchildren. That morning in South Bend, I made the decision to inquire about updating and publishing it.

For me, as for the fictional character Forrest Gump, the years have been eventful, filled with recollections of education, marriage, children, work, and much more. I have been at the scene of a few history-making events, including the assassination of President John F. Kennedy and the Oklahoma City bombing. In the meantime, my life in the Southwest and in the Washington, DC, area brought me into contact with several notable people. Most of them were casual acquaintances or the result of one-time encounters; a few became close friends.

My background, including my political activity, participation in the civil-rights movement, support of Planned Parenthood, and professional work as a campaign manager and consultant, as well as my later work running a family business, offered me unusual opportunities. I was able to observe America as it changed profoundly from unity to division and perhaps back to a nascent movement toward understanding.

My vantage point has been one of a spear carrier standing in the wings of the drama or one among those who comprise society's "middle management," whose efforts keep things moving. I am neither journalist nor historian; I'm simply a writer; and this book tells what I have seen.

Chapter 1

AWAKENING IN THE GREAT DEPRESSION

FORMER UNITED STATES Senator Fred R. Harris once told me that to him, poverty had a brown taste. What I remember of the 1930s was a brown time like the sepia of the pictures my mother hung in the upstairs hall, including photographs of some of the scenes Thomas Moran painted: El Capitan Mountain in Yosemite and Yellowstone Falls. The tinted paper was more real to me than colorful oil on canvas. I also recalled the tanned leather of the cavalry boots and the Sam Brown belts of National Guardsmen, the khaki of CCC uniforms, the vehicles at the Armory, the shirts of the Highway Patrol, and the sienna insignias on their wide-brimmed hats.

Everything in our 1933 world of Oklahoma City was tinted with the brown of the dust bowl. The hard-packed earth, often cracked by the heat like old pottery, was too solid to fill the sky. Then years of drought brought swirling clouds of loosened soil broken by hundreds of plows. Dust rose up in the spring and rolled across the prairies. Dust, tinted faintly pink from red clay, filtered through windows, collecting in a thick pall on the ebony surface of the Mason and Hamlin grand piano in our living room. Dust filled the sky, necessitating streetlamps to be turned on in the daytime. Dust permeated the copper-colored velvet draperies; its odor was everywhere.

In clear weather in those days before air conditioning, when it was warm and the windows were open, I pressed my face against the screen until it marked the end of my nose with a crosshatch, and I breathed in the powdery smell. In winter, the steam-filled radiators gave off waves of dusty heat. It was familiar, it was home, and it was Oklahoma.

Most of my life was centered around my home, my grandparents who lived three blocks away, and Lincoln School, the elementary school that was five blocks directly south of our home. The public schools in Oklahoma City, at least for white children, were perhaps as good as schools anywhere. School began at age five with half-day kindergarten, and by the fourth grade, music and art classes were available for everyone. The school library was a treasure trove. The teachers were well-trained and likable, and the principal, Ethel M. Liebhart, was enough of a disciplinarian to maintain iron control and kind enough to be admired. She knew the name of every student in the large school and more about their backgrounds than most teachers did.

But in Oklahoma it was still the Great Depression. The impact of the "dust bowl" was everywhere, not just in the curiously pink skies when hot winds blew. Most of the children in my class were from families who felt the brunt of the ongoing economic crisis. Several had moved often during the past years; some had gone with their families to California only to come back to Oklahoma. There they found, like the Joads, that the Golden State wasn't the land of golden opportunity.

California became an object of some derision for us, not because of its job market, but because of its prejudice against

Oklahomans. Students from Oklahoma were invariably put back a grade when they arrived in California. We supposed education officials based that on an assumption that Oklahomans were not as well educated as their own students.

Invariably, when the students, whose fathers could not find work there, returned to Oklahoma, they really were badly behind. This was because the overcrowded California school system was unable to cope with an influx of children. In Oklahoma, our teachers grumbled, and our parents clucked over this state of affairs. The rest of us went right ahead with learning.

I was the rich kid in the class. It was not a subject for teasing, but the quiet envy disturbed me. I began to be aware of examples of inequity around me. With no air conditioning anywhere but in movie theaters, schoolrooms in spring and fall were hot. One of my friends had only a single summer dress. It was jade green cotton, printed with small flowers and washed slightly gray. Her mother must have washed and starched and ironed this dress every night. Each morning, she appeared at school scrupulously clean. Its puffed sleeves were pressed into the stiff shape of paper lanterns, and a knife crease circled them where they had been folded against the ironing board to press the gathers.

I could not avoid seeing the differences between my classmates' worn and patched clothing and mine. Other girls' good dresses were bought at JC Penny's instead of the department stores where mother purchased mine. They brought lunches to school in brown paper sacks and carefully counted out pennies to purchase candy after school. I had a prepaid card for a hot lunch every day and received an allowance of a quarter each week.

Schoolmates asked the occasional diffident question. "Do you really have golden gates in your house?" In a redecoration scheme, mother had replaced the forest green carpet in the hall and stairway with a gold carpet, woven with fronds of wheat in it. The verdigris wrought-iron banister and balusters, as well as the gates leading to the living room, had been repainted with gilt paint.

I often played on the Italian marble floor of the living room that was covered by my mother's favorite Chinese rugs, and the gates became part of my fantasies, metamorphosing into elevator doors or castle gates as story lines dictated. But I could only answer "yes" to their embarrassing questions. These differences between me and the other students became a point of sensitivity for me.

One of the things I did not share with my friends was political beliefs. None of us as children had real political convictions, but each of us became a reflection of the ideas expressed by our parents. Franklin D. Roosevelt was President. He was elected in the fall of 1932, and his inauguration took place fifty-five days before I was born. He would continue as president of the United States until shortly before my twelfth birthday. He was not admired in my home, but he was a hero to most of the parents of my friends. The United States at the time of Roosevelt's election was a time warp away from the United States of today. At that time, bank deposits were not insured in any way. There was no social security. Whatever people saved for retirement—if they could save anything at all—was in stocks and bonds, in a bank account, in thrift institutions referred to by my grandparents as "The Building and Loan," or in postal savings bonds. The nearly destitute kept cash buried in a coffee tin in the backyard, between the mattress and bedsprings, or in a sugar bowl.

Local and national news was spread by word of mouth, the radio, or the newspaper. The *Oklahoma City Times* was delivered each afternoon, and my father sat in his red leather overstuffed chair in the library to read it after supper in the evenings. My older brother, Thurman, would go to his room to listen to the radio, and mother went to hers to read. As a toddler, I would lie on the silky pile of the blue Chinese rug in the library and play with toys and sometimes build a house out of the hinged brass fire screen. I also loved to look at the cartoons on the back page of the paper, the editorial page. The drawings were more interesting to me than the photos on the front page, so I thought the newspaper should be read back to front. My father explained to me that the most important news was on the front page where the print was larger and signaled to the reader what was important in the news.

One evening, when I crawled up onto his lap while he was reading the front page, I saw a picture of a child sitting on a long flight of steps and crying. The child's terror was apparent to me, and then I noticed bodies lying scattered here and there on the steps.

"But, where's his mother?" I asked.

"I don't know," was his simple answer.

"What's happening?"

He explained carefully to me that the little boy was Chinese and that his country and another country called Japan were at war. He told me in a war people are killed, sometimes even mothers and children. "But" he said, "China is very far away, too far for any of this to worry you." Within three years, the haunted terror of the little boy in Nanking would be as familiar and as close to me as our Chinese rug.

Chapter 2

WHAT I LEARNED AT MY MOTHER'S KNEE

MY INTRODUCTION TO intolerance was as casual as my introduction to war. I'm not sure how much of my first brush with prejudice I actually remember, or how much I was told later. One summer when I was about four, my family planned a vacation in Florida. Some of the memories are vivid: being stung by a bee, seeing the Swanee River from the song I had learned. There were the orange groves, the horse-drawn carriages in St. Augustine, the beach where my grandfather built me a "bathtub," and especially the miniature lighthouse at the hotel where we stayed.

The hotel was not the hotel where we had originally planned to stay. In preparation for the trip, my father wrote to the Roney Plaza Hotel in Miami. He received a polite reply that they were "terribly sorry, but our clientele is restricted to gentiles." My father was furious. His background was German-Lutheran, but his name was Morris Myers. He was angry about both the assumption and the policy.

Mother was the epitome of a generation of women I would come to call the "Main Street girls" after the women described in Sinclair Lewis' novel *Main Street*. Mother and her friends were the first generation of college-educated women, and most of them came from middle-class backgrounds, a rung up from the working class their fathers had sprung from. With their improvement in status and education came a hunger for something beyond housewifery and childbearing while they still fervently desired all the good things that made houses beautiful. They created study clubs and played bridge, and their conversation was a mix of gossip, public affairs, recipes, and discussions of recent books.

Mother loved to play bridge, and she and her friends played every week. Occasionally, when school was out or I had the sniffles, I would hang about listening to their conversations. One conversation I overheard struck me as curious. The women were discussing an acquaintance whose husband was Jewish. The couple had just purchased a home in a prestigious neighborhood. One of the women remarked, "I didn't know they could buy there." The conversation continued with a discussion of "gentlemen's agreements." Later, I would come to know the practice as redlining.

I particularly remember another conversation because of the vehemence with which my mother defended her position. John Steinbeck's *Grapes of Wrath* had just been published. The other three women were indignant at what they considered Steinbeck's condescending attitude toward Oklahoma. "But, have you read it?" my mother insisted. They had not.

"Well, read it. It's the Californians who come out badly. The Oklahomans are the heroes."

The other three retreated into silence; they were either unconvinced or perhaps had resolved to read the book. Their conversation was puzzling and instructive to me. When I finally read the book in college, I thought my mother had had the best of the argument. But I remembered the sense of indignation and insecurity expressed in the voices of other women when they discussed the book. Their insecurity,

I would conclude when I grew up, consisted of equal parts megalomania, paranoia, and a determined anti-intellectualism that still pervades my home state. The indignation sprang from a conviction that everyone and everything Oklahoman is looked down upon by the rest of the nation. It is a kind of "What makes you think you're better than I am?" attitude, which ignores the fact that most of the rest of the nation has no opinion about the state at all. For most people, "Oklahoma" usually brings to mind only the musical play, football, or, unfortunately, the bombing of the Murrah Building.

In the 1930s, the United States was a creditor nation, so there was money in the bank. With no other resources, the government became the employer of last resort. Thus were born the CCC and the WPA. Regardless of my dad's epithet for the Works Project Administration, "We Piddle Always," what I saw was the construction of numerous public buildings in Oklahoma City by the WPA.

New buildings of all kinds were constructed in the 1920s and 1930s. The city took on a sleek modernistic look that was clean and pleasing. Two of the buildings were more than thirty stories tall and stood across the street from each other so the profile of the city rose to a single center. According to my mother, airline pilots regarded the Oklahoma City skyline as one of the most beautiful in the country.

Government provided other new things important to me. There was something called the school-lunch program, and I was aware that it paid for meals for some of my friends and classmates, but considerable care was used to conceal the identity of the "underprivileged," as the jargon of that day went.

Poverty was such a fact of life in the 1930s that it often went unremarked until it appeared in a more personal form. Our house was only two long blocks from the Santa Fe tracks. Thousands of men rode the rails during those years, looking for work or simply surviving in the hobo camps and collectively sharing the food they had earned or stolen. It was a rough life, mostly lived by young men forced to be itinerant simply to find scarce work rather than to resort to crime.

Occasionally our doorbell would ring, and a man would be standing there dressed in worn clothes and usually wearing a workman's sixpenny cap. He would ask for food, and my mother always made the stranger a sandwich. She did not skimp but would cut thick slices of meatloaf and add French's mustard and lettuce to the white bread. I remember peeking from the library window, watching a man sit down quietly on the front porch and eat one of those sandwiches. When I questioned Mother, she said, "He is just a man without a job and doesn't have money to buy food, so he has to beg for his bread. Perhaps he is off looking for work to support children at home."

I was an infant when Roosevelt declared the nation's bank holiday, but my mother told the story of our maid Caroline overhearing Mother and Dad discuss the crisis during dinner. All bank accounts were frozen so no one had any cash, and at the time, people didn't know how long the banks would be closed.

The Post Office used to issue savings bonds, called Postal Savings, and since they were not part of the banking industry, they were still available. As she cleared the supper dishes, Caroline offered to loan the cash she could still retrieve from her post office account to my father if he needed it. He thanked her and said he hoped the financial standstill would not be long enough to require such generosity. My mother always told this story with some amusement, given the difference in the financial circumstances of the maid and her employer. My father was deeply touched by the offer.

Postal Savings were to play a part in another drama involving Caroline and the family. Caroline was a Negro, a universally used term back then. Black people lived south of Tenth Street and east of the Santa Fe tracks. I seem always to have known this as fact. Grover Cleveland Copeland, known as "Money," was also Black; he mowed our lawn and weeded the flowerbeds. When he needed extra cash, he washed our navy-blue Packard. One day he came to work with gashes on his back where his wife had taken an ice pick to him. Mother discussed this on the phone with my grandmother. I was fascinated; it was the first time I had ever seen the results of physical violence.

When I was about five and allowed to cross streets, a Black family moved into the garage of one of the houses across from our house. They had two children, one a girl just my age. I was delighted. My brother Thurman had dozens of boys in the neighborhood to play with, but I was the only girl. It was summer, and the girl and I played on the porch. She had shyly crossed the street and introduced herself. After a while we went to where her family was living. The garage had a tamped dirt floor, a mattress, and a small kerosene stove. I remember the little girl was clean and neat, and her hair was tightly braided. I brought paper dolls to play with.

When I told my mother about my new friend, all she said was, "You can't play with her anymore." To my anguished question "Why?" she just shook her head, ending any discussion. The family did not stay long in the neighborhood.

Our maid Caroline had almost complete charge of me. When I was two, Mother began to lose a great deal of weight. My grandfather became concerned and insisted she go to the Mayo Clinic. She had what was then called a nervous breakdown. Caroline stayed with us during that time. I have vague memories of her cooking and singing to me. I have wondered if it was from her that I learned the habit of singing spirituals to myself when I am troubled. When I was three or four, Mother fired Caroline. "Let her go," was the phrase she used. Years later she told me it was because Caroline was ill, with syphilis as it turned out, and in some overly protective way, Mother was afraid the disease would transmit to us.

Regardless of the firing, when Caroline got into trouble, it was my mother she called. And it certainly was trouble. She had a common-law husband, "not married with words," as she explained. It seems her husband had cashed in all her precious postal savings bonds and spent them on what Caroline described as a "yella gal." Caroline's husband drove a taxi. One evening when he picked her up, Caroline got into the back seat and asked him to drive out to Belle Isle Lake. After he parked at the lake, she confronted him about the empty savings account, and he readily admitted his waywardness. When he turned to start the car, she calmly shot him, quite effectively, in the back of the head. She left the gun in the car and somehow got to a telephone. The best Mother could do was to call her brother, my Uncle Charles, who was a new graduate of the University of Oklahoma's School of Law.

Fortunately, one of his law classmates worked in the district attorney's office. The two of them went before the judge and pleaded her case on manslaughter charges. The judge was appalled, but when the DA's office declined to press any other charges, there was little he could do. "Gentlemen," he protested, "this woman committed cold-blooded, calculated murder." The most he could do was to sentence her to the maximum-security prison at McAlester, where she spent her time cooking for the warden. She was paroled in the early 1940s and went to California to work in the defense plants.

Justice was either unavailable or uneven for Black people. Oklahoma was settled equally by Northerners like my family, who primarily followed the oil industry there, and by Southern ranchers and farmers. The ethos of the state was

Southern. Nowhere did the Ku Klux Klan ride harder than in Oklahoma. The Klan even burned a cross on the lawn of the University of Oklahoma's President because his wife was a Catholic. Protestant fundamentalists, especially Southern Baptists, wielded enormous political power. What the judge and the attorneys knew in Caroline's case was that, like most people of color, she had no recourse in the civil courts to recoup any losses. Blacks had their own lawyers, often good ones, but courts had no patience with their cases.

Riding in the back of the bus, drinking from separate water fountains, using separate toilets. and being relegated to the balconies of the movie theaters (if they would admit you at all) were minor irritations compared with separate schools and housing, scant justice, and an inability to get a housing loan. During urban renewal in the 1960s and the 1970s, the white community would come to appreciate one of the unintended consequences of this last indignity. When the city finally co-opted and tore down a large part of the Black part of town in the 1970s to build the Presbyterian Hospital complex, there were many lucky inhabitants who did not rent but owned their own properties outright, bought with hard-earned savings. The city had to pay the inhabitants fair-market value. The former residents promptly took their cash and bought or built where they pleased. Integrated housing in Oklahoma City took place in one swift and very expensive action for the white community. In its wake it left pockets of devastation and disappearing business for much of the Black community.

The city was then and still is roughly divided into quarters. Instead of the Capitol's being the hub of the quadrants, the old intersection of Main Street and Broadway became the point of division for numbering the streets. However, two physical barriers are actually more important: the Santa Fe tracks that run north and south through the city and the North Canadian River that bisects it from west to east. The northwest section of the city always dominated commerce and politics. For most citizens from the more affluent portion of the city, nothing existed south of the river. What was once a poor and lower-middle-class working section of the city is now huge and stretches from what was once called Sand Town on the river to some extremely affluent areas. Most of south Oklahoma City gave up long ago and formed its own alliances and a Chamber of Commerce. Occasionally one of the "south towners" made enough money to move to Nichols Hills, the exclusive enclave of the elite in the northwest. I grew up on the East Side of town, the most beautiful section of the city with its rolling hills and trees, the graceful Capitol building, the zoo, the racetrack, and the Cowboy Hall of Fame.

But the Black families who lived on our side of town were in the restricted area south of Northeast Tenth Street and the Canadian River, the only place they were permitted to own property. It was impossible to grow up in the Jim Crow South without internalizing a great deal of racism. The area below Tenth Street was casually called "Nigger Town." I never saw Black children, except for the little girl who lived across the street. Caroline and Lily, who cleaned for my grandmother and for us, arrived from the shadow land in the mornings to work and disappeared into it at night.

No African American residents shopped downtown or went to the movie theaters I attended, but I saw them in their own sections of the train depot or on the rear seats of streetcars. Often, I thought they were outlandishly dressed; my mother said that it was a matter of taste. Perhaps, but it was also often the result of having no choice when it came to donated clothing. This never crossed either of our minds. Most of all there was the acknowledged sense of danger that was an almost tangible barrier, like an electric fence that seemed to make an area safe for them and not for me. Conversely, there was wariness in the eyes of the Black folks I passed on the street when they were north of Tenth Street who told me that they were always on guard.

By the end of the 1930s I had learned a lot of lessons in sociology. I learned somewhere in the world there was a war that killed mothers and left babies crying on stone steps, that national economics could affect those closest to me and that the government could be a major instrument in how the economy worked in the lives of ordinary people and could even change the way my hometown looked. Finally, in the society in which I lived people considered Jews to be different from and less than Christians and that society made Blacks live in segregation.

I did not question any of these things, but they troubled me. Yet I would have been surprised had I known the faraway war would burst on all of us like a bomb and that I would spend most of my life trying to make some sense out of government and its role in the lives of people. In the 1960s, I would come to know some Jews well and would also become friends with some of the children who were growing up in the shadows south of Tenth Street.

Somewhere in these shadows, there was a boy who was befriended by the son of the conductor of the first Oklahoma City Symphony and was encouraged by him and by his own family to look beyond the city. The boy, a native of Oklahoma City, would leave in the early 1930s for other cities and, like so many, make his way to Harlem where he would write the first major chronicle of growing up Black in the brown time of the 1930s. He would also write about the shadows in our hometown. Somewhere, eight blocks south of me, Ralph Ellison was becoming a man.

Chapter 3

ROOTS

MY HUSBAND AND I represent two different patterns of settlement in America. My family, northerners from New York, Pennsylvania, and the old Northwest states of Ohio and Indiana, is an example of one pattern. A cousin of my father, an active member of the DAR, traced his mother's family all the way back to the Mayflower. Protestant and French Huguenot influences were predominant in the clan. In contrast, my father's father was born in the United States only because he came along after my grandfather's parents and his older brother left Germany and sailed to America.

My mother's maternal family, like my father's, hailed from eighteenth-century Scotland. It was German-Hessian on the paternal side and similarly polyglot on my grandmother's side, but her own father was born in Hythe, County Kent, England. In contrast, my husband's family settled in Virginia during the mid-seventeenth century and mostly retained their British heritage. The Taliaferro family traces back to 1555 when Venetian traders left Italy to settle in Stepney, near London. The single progenitor, Robert, left England in 1666 to establish a trading company in Virginia. By the time Robert Taliaferro came to Virginia, the British had dropped the Italian pronunciation and scrambled the name, as they did with so many others. For instance, the French name Cholmondeley is now Chumley, Beauchamp became Beecham, and Taliaferro is now pronounced "Toliver." My sons still carefully retain both the Italian spelling and the British pronunciation, and I answer to anything close to Tal-ee-ah-ferro. An interesting development came when my husband and I were researching his family in county courthouses in Virginia. He found a will in which the name was written one way in the granting clause and another way in the habendum clause.

A second exception on my children's paternal side was made when their great-grandfather, a great-great-grandnephew of President Madison, left his school and his home in North Texas where the family lived after the Civil War. He crossed the Red River to haul wood for members of the Choctaw Nation. He was forced to do so because the family went bankrupt after the Civil War. Eventually, great grandpa married a woman in Oklahoma who was part Choctaw and part Irish. This allowed him to stay in Indian territory, buy land, and raise a family. His son, my father-in-law, was born early enough to appear on the Daws Commission rolls as a tribal member.

This fraction of his Indian blood appeared on the DNA test of my elder son, who laughingly told me it registered as Athabaskan, a far cry from the Muskogean-speaking Choctaws. I had an advantage, growing up in Oklahoma, to be aware of the subtle differences in some four hundred-plus tribes occupying land in the state. Sociologists try to group them by language groups including Anishinaabe, Muskogean Sioux, and Athabaskan. We knew them by whatever tribe an individual claimed to be. As grade-school students, we had to learn the history of the five tribes that were moved to Oklahoma from the east coast, and to memorize the names of the tribes' principal chiefs at the time of their removal—e.g., "Pushmataha" and "John Ross."

Being Native American was a badge of honor. My mother's best friend was Cherokee. I once asked her, "Aunt Lynne, are you a *wild* Indian?" She and my mother both laughed, perhaps thinking of a reference to their behavior in the roaring 20s. I could never understand the deep resentment against Native Americans I encountered in other parts of the country. In Oklahoma, "they" were "us." Years later I would come to understand the deeply populist strain in Oklahoma, which was settled during the last ten years of the nineteenth century. The ideas of self-reliance and distrust of government were strong influences within the young state. This distrust of authority resulted in the composition of the longest constitution of any state in the union. It includes every law the framers thought might ever be considered, using explicit constitutional language. Consequently, initiatives and referendums have always been popular, and citizens are amazed to find that there are states in the Union that prohibit such exercises in what most Oklahomans would consider "real democracy."

As in Australia, settlement brought more than our share of the restless and eccentric, some of whom no other community would want. In a discussion over lunch an Oklahoma State Senator once remarked to me, "America was settled by a lot of misfits from Europe, and Oklahoma was settled by some who were misfits among misfits." Although an overstatement, it has a grain of truth. Many who came to the state were simply looking for opportunity, and some found it.

My grandfathers were examples of each group. My mother's father, Charles R. Stewart, left school at fourteen and never again had any formal education. A native of Pennsylvania, he began his career along with an older brother digging ditches for the Eureka Pipeline Company. Eventually he married his childhood sweetheart, my grandmother, and moved to West Virginia, following the oil industry. There he worked on the first major oil pipeline built in this country, near Cairo, West Virginia. He and Stella Godfrey had three children while they lived there. My mother was the eldest, and Grandmother named her Crete. We were never sure why the name was chosen, as it apparently had nothing to do with the Greek island. The most likely reason was President Garfield's wife was named Lucretia and called "Crete." Shortening a name for my grandmother was easily done, since her own name given at baptism was Estella, which she never used. My mother's sister, Aunt Bernice, was two years younger than my mother, and her brother, my Uncle Charles, was ten years younger.

By 1911 my grandfather came with my grandmother and three of their four children to Healdton, Oklahoma. My mother's youngest sibling, my Aunt Virgina, was born in Oklahoma. The family then moved to Ardmore and later to Oklahoma City. The Eureka company became a part of Magnolia Oil and was subsequently merged with Mobil. My grandfather ended his career as head of the pipeline division of Magnolia for Oklahoma, southern Kansas, and parts of north Texas. His older brother left the ditches behind to become President of Magnolia and sat on the board of Mobil.

The romance of the turn of the century and the first fifty years of this millennium may be exaggerated, but it was truly a time when you could do whatever you were "man enough" to do. The necessary elements were physical strength and endurance coupled with the intelligence and imagination needed to develop a vast land. Much business was done on trust, and a man's word and handshake were his bond. Few pushed the boundaries, partly because it wasn't necessary and partly because the weight of public opinion would ensure you would never again be trusted. Shame was a community weapon.

My father's father, James Myers, was quite different. The son of a German immigrant, he was reared in rural Indiana. As a young man he taught school in a Swiss-German-speaking community because he could understand what the children said. Dad said the Myers immigrant was a cobbler from Wittenberg, Germany, but a family history proves it was actually Wurttemberg in Bavaria. Regardless, they were deeply influenced by the two great institutions represented by Wittenberg: the university and Martin Luther. Lutherans to the core, they became Methodists when they emigrated. One of my grandfather's brothers was a noted Methodist minister in Indiana. But it was Luther and his intellectual independence that impressed the family so deeply they retained a legend that an ancestor once hid Luther in her attic when Roman Catholic authorities were searching for him. Although there is no corroboration for the story, my father recounted it to me often and with great conviction.

Grandfather Myers was, by most standards, a ne'er-do-well. He ended his life in the company of a whiskey bottle after having careers as farmer, woolen mill and sawmill owner, and proprietor of a small business making cement blocks. Disaster always seemed to follow him. The competition of cheap woolens, produced in quantity by the Hudson's Bay Company, drove him and his brother out of the wool business in Indiana. A flood on the Tennessee River washed away his sawmill, just as the Studebaker Wagon Company had given him a contract to produce whiffletrees. A "whiffletree," sometimes called a "singletree," was a part of the apparatus that attached horses to a wagon. His adventure into fabricating cement blocks was always referred to as "a good idea whose time had not yet come." He died just before

I was born but left his grandchildren two legacies: alcoholism and a love of learning and education.

He was twice married and twice widowed; his first wife, my grandmother, was descended from the Bradfords who came to America on the Mayflower. She died from having a tapeworm when my father was a year old. She had acquired the disease when she would eat bits of raw meat to help her chronic anemia. Father Myers had three sons. The first he named Franklin after Benjamin Franklin. The second he named Homer Milton after two of his favorite poets. My father's real name was Morse (for Samuel F.B.) and Thurman (for some admired German ancestor or a god). When he was still a boy, my father changed Morse to Morris because he hated being addressed as "Morsey." Ironically, his granddaughters would lovingly dub him Morsey as soon as they could talk.

His eldest son, my Uncle Frank, was a graduate of Vanderbilt and a doctor. I remember him as a lonely, morose man. He was a surgeon who served in World War I at Chateau Thierry in what would be called a MASH unit in the Korean War. He never got over the experience of the war, but he did continue to practice as a surgeon in Tulsa until his death in 1942. I still have an Iron Cross he took from a dead German officer brought into the unit; its enamel and steel were as crisp as the day it had been awarded.

Uncle Homer graduated from Purdue University and went on to MIT. He worked until his retirement as an engineer for General Electric in Boston. My father took his first year of college at the University of Wisconsin and loved the school but hated the cold. By 1909, his sophomore year, his father (my grandfather) was living in Shawnee, Oklahoma, so my father earned a Bachelor of Science degree at the University of Oklahoma in Norman. He was awarded the first ever Master of Science degree in chemistry at the university.

But business was my father's first love. By the time he graduated, he had bought an old house directly across from the University's chemistry building. In it he opened a bookstore and a sandwich shop and called it the Varsity Shop. He had spotted the property while working in the chemistry lab directly across the street from it. From there he observed the students had to walk a half mile to town on a boardwalk to get their books and supplies.

We still have a copy of the first invoice he received for supplies to stock the Varsity Shop. Smoking goods, especially cigars, were a major item. On the bottom of the invoice he wrote, "This is the first of the nest egg for my grandchildren." He was a cautious businessman. "The pace of business is always slow," he would tell me. "Don't get in a hurry." Seventy years later, I took over and expanded the property. I have often thought it would have been better if I had been in more of a hurry to start a career in business, but his advice was still good.

My family has been engaged in the oil business for five generations. Albert Godfrey, my British great-grandfather, who was farming in western Pennsylvania, became fascinated by Colonel Drake's discovery of how to extract oil. In pursuit of the wealth it offered, he left the family to travel to Texas shortly after reports of the discovery of the Spindletop well near Houston in 1901. A relatively young man, he was not there long before he tragically died from what was termed "apoplexy," but could have been a stroke, a heart attack, or heat exhaustion.

In the next generation, Albert's oldest daughter, my grandmother, married Charles Stewart, who was equally avid to leave the farm to pursue the oil business. When their daughter married, my dad was already engaged in the business. Mother kept his books, and we still have ledgers with her exquisite handwriting and neat numbers. Before my parents married in 1922, my father left Norman to go to Oklahoma City and got into the oil business with his brother-in-law, Homer Keegan and his best friend Willard Miller. He had already sold the bookstore portion of the Varsity Shop. The Varsity Shop endured as a campus restaurant and gathering place until the 1930s on what had become known as Campus Corner in Norman. The building was then renovated and rented to Kerr's department store, one of the larger stores in Oklahoma City. Its owners wanted a location in Norman. The property remained a retail rental store through the years, and it has been successful in riding out the ups and downs in the economy along with the advent of the automobile and the development of shopping malls.

My father had a reputation for being knowledgeable, driving a hard bargain, and always playing fair. In addition, he had a quiet compassion. During the hard days of the 1930s, he would often buy oil and gas mineral interests in areas he did not particularly want from someone who needed the money. But he also received good advice. My father's best friend was "Uncle Willard" Miller. He was married to my mother's closest friend and was a superb geologist. It was his knowledge that guided my father's purchases. During this time, my father began to play the stock market, cautiously and shrewdly and with such intensity that on the morning my mother was in labor with me and the nurse was trying to get in touch with him, my mother instructed her to call Fenner and Beane. Indeed, he was sitting in the old "bucket shop" watching the tape at Merrill Lynch, Pierce, Fenner & Beane, as it was then known.

My father shared an office with his brother-in-law, Homer Keegan, the husband of my father's half-sister, Eva. Homer had a job as a land man, buying leases for the Indian Territory Illuminating Oil Company. He taught my father the business, and together they "blocked up" the first leases in the Oklahoma City field. The leases eventually led to the drilling of the wells, some of which still surrounded the capital when I was growing up. In the early 1940s, my father formed a partnership called the MBK Drilling Company and went into the producing side of the oil business. "M" was for Myers, "B" was for Harry Brown, and "K" was for my uncle Homer Keegan. Harry Brown was what my mother called a "plunger," but most people called a "wildcatter." He aggressively acquired leases, especially in Texas, whereas my father had always kept his ownership limited to Oklahoma. Harry led the operations, and my dad led the business end of the venture. My uncle eventually decided it was all too dicey for him and let the others buy him out.

Harry lived in Tulsa. As a little girl, I remember going downtown with my father to meet Harry for lunch at a restaurant that had a bar. Perhaps I got squirmy as they discussed business, because my real memory was that Harry kept me happy with Dentyne chewing gum and fed me a new piece whenever the old one had lost its cinnamon flavor. I suppose Harry handled the drilling part as expertly as he managed me, until the day in 1944 when we received the news that Harry had died of a sudden heart attack. This left my father as the sole operator of the company. Not only was he not a driller by trade, but Harry's death left the shares of the stock in the hands of two women—Harry's widow and his secretary. It did not help that there was always suspicion that Harry's secretary occupied a more central place in his life than as an employee.

Dad put the company up for sale. Negotiations were long and involved. It took more than a year for the assets to be split between Big Chief Drilling and what was then known as Kerlyn Oil. Kerlyn was an exploration company owned by US Senator Robert S. Kerr and a man named Lynn. Neither Big Chief nor Kerlyn had the funds to buy MBK outright.

As it happened, shortly after the sale the first twenty-one wells came in good. It was the opening of the Sprayberry Field in West Texas near Midland, and it helped build the Kerr-McGee Oil Company. In 1963, when my father was in the hospital recovering from his first stroke, he and I walked to the end of the corridor to see what was happening at the First Baptist Church. We watched as President Kennedy's limousine pulled up for him to attend Senator Kerr's funeral.

"That was the worst business decision I ever made," my father remarked. I believe that was the first time he ever referred to the sale to Kerlyn. I replied, "I don't think so. I think the strain would have killed you years ago." Then I added, "Maybe you should have taken some stock though." He explained that he knew the senator was much more interested in what was going on in Washington and had no time to oversee a large company. In addition, he wondered about the ability of those who were running the company at the time of the sale. As it happened, in 1939 the senator had hired Dean McGee away from Phillips, and he was soon running the operation. It was McGee who really built the company.

Nevertheless, the sale made our family comfortably wealthy, and my father's other investments in minerals made it possible for all of us to have the basic necessities while we worked in other employment. Watching what great wealth can do to some families, I have never regretted the outcome. The only other reference to the sale I remember my father making was to admonish me, "Never get into the production side of the business, and never take a working interest in a well instead of a straight lease." When I took over running the business, I found that making money and giving it away was my idea of fun. If I had any regrets about the sale of MBK, I was only sorry that I didn't have more to give away.

Chapter 4

WAR

BY THE END of the 1930s, the war in Europe arrived at the shores of Great Britain. Churchill was universally admired, and his ringing oratory was as familiar to American ears as the polished phrases of FDR. It was a time of passionate political division, not just between Republican and Democrat but between those who were opposed to going to war and those who were in favor of it. Far below the consciousness of most Americans were the actions of those who approved of what was going on in Europe. "Mussolini made the railroads run on time," was a familiar talking point. On the surface, America appeared to be a wholehearted ally of Britian and Free France. After all, there was the Lend-Lease Act that allowed the United States to provide aid to the Allied powers.

It was my mother's remarks about a certain Father Coughlin that caught my ear. He became a radio personality, one who supported what Hitler was doing in Germany, and he hoped to convince the public to adopt an ultraconservative agenda for America. Although she was a Republican and a conservative, Mother had contempt for the man who used his radio program to broadcast antisemitic commentary and supported some of the policies of Nazi Germany and Fascist Italy. I would think of those spokespersons later in the 1950s with the emergence of the John Birch Society. The America First attitude never quite disappeared.

Most Americans tried to turn a blind eye to our inevitable involvement, even though programs such as Lend-Lease had begun and our factories were producing armaments for our allies. Many young Americans, rather than waiting for the war to come to them, volunteered to fight in Britain or to join the French Foreign Legion. Also, the United States Army began to call up its reserves.

In April of 1940, a year and a half before Pearl Harbor, mother's brother, my Uncle Charles, received notice that his ROTC commission as a Second Lieutenant was being activated and he was to report for duty. Charles had joined the ROTC in college because cadets rode horses. We were not at war, but dinner at my grandmother's house the night before he left had the same sad apprehension, I am sure, that afflicts all households with men going off to war.

I have vivid memories of that night. Those of us who lived in Oklahoma City gathered at my grandmother's house for a farewell supper. After dinner my uncle went upstairs to write some letters. As he sat at his desk, I sat in a chair behind him and drew his picture on some blank sheets of paper he gave me. The back of the bentwood chair was behind him, and the student lamp with the green glass shade, oval and bright as a jellybean, was to his left. His shirtsleeves were rolled up, and a cotton handkerchief poked a triangle out of his hip pocket. On the corner of the desk was a device that fascinated me: it was a porcelain trough, perhaps three inches by an inch and a half. A porcelain wheel was mounted on a chrome-plated axis and was situated in the middle of the trough.

"What does it do?" I asked.

"It licks your stamps for you," he said. "Go get a little bit of water, and I'll show you."

I went into the bathroom and put just a little water in the bottom of the trough. When I carried it back to his desk, he spun the wheel until it was moist. Then he tore off a strip of three-cent stamps and handed them to me. "Now run them across the wheel." He let me put stamps on all the letters he had written. "Let's see what you've drawn," he said. When he looked at my picture, he took it downstairs to show it to everyone and delightedly pointed out the handkerchief in his back pocket, turning around to prove the detail was accurate.

As pleased as I was with the attention, I couldn't shake my sense of foreboding. I thought I might never see him again. The question in my mind was "Will he ever come back?" As it turned out, he never saw the kind of action many saw on D-Day, but he landed in a subsequent wave and was close enough to be fired upon during his tour of duty in the European theater of operations.

The next time I did see my Uncle Charles, he was in full summer uniform, and his Second Lieutenant's bars were on the tabs of his khaki shirt. We went to Galveston, Texas, for a short vacation. There he was assigned to the Coastal Artillery to teach young men, most of whom did not speak English, how to fire the cannons that were supposed to safeguard our southern coast. Practice on the firing range consisted of trying to hit a target that was towed behind a small plane on a long cable. The plane was not a drone; it was flown by a real pilot. The most difficult part of his job, he explained to us, was communicating with the South Texas trainees since English was his only language. "No, no," he would gesture wildly and shout. "Not at the plane—at the target!" During the time he was training troops he named a barrage balloon after me. I never saw the "Janet" balloon, a small, fat, blimp. Alas, the Janet balloon became a casualty, not of war but of a lightning bolt that struck its tail.

Later in the war, Charles' legal background put him into intelligence as a liaison officer. He went to England, then to France a few days after June 6, 1944, then finally crossed France to get to Germany. He received the Chevalier Légion d'Honneur from the French government for his role in helping to set up the military government in the French sector. He did not think this was much of an accomplishment. I greatly admired the beautiful medal, and years later I asked his daughter about it. She had never heard the story nor seen the medal. Perhaps he simply disposed of it at some point.

Probably he considered his part in the recovery of art from the Reichstag Museum much more important and a lot more fun. He was one of the officers who oversaw the removal and return to Berlin of famous works of art that had been buried for safekeeping in a salt mine in southern Germany. I remember him saying, "I held Rembrandt's *Man with the Golden Helmet* in my hands."

Any pretense we were only "studying" war, in the words of the old gospel hymn, came to an end on a sunny Sunday in December 1941. That morning, I went to church with my family. Afterward we stopped at Bishop's Cafe for lunch. As the adults talked, my attention wandered to my surroundings. The restaurant had several dining rooms. At the busy Sunday noon hour, we were seated in the room closest to the street. A long lunch counter of dark wood ran along the length of the north wall, and the south wall was lined with booths made of the same wood. A deep header at the ceiling was papered with images of sailing vessels that figured in American history, including the *Nina, Pinta*, and *Santa Maria*, and my favorite because of its romantic name, the *Half Moon*. Waitresses bustled about in black uniforms topped by crisp white cotton aprons and tiny matching crownless caps designed to keep their hair in place. My attention also wandered to conversations at the surrounding tables. The restaurant was only three blocks from the building that housed the *Daily Oklahoman* and the *Oklahoma City Times*. Two men in the booth behind me were having a conversation. I couldn't make out what it was about, but the serious tone was inescapable.

The waitress brought a pirate's chest full of cheap toys, most marked "Made in Japan," to the table after dessert. They were gifts for any of the children who were under twelve to select. I don't remember what I chose or what movie we walked to at the Criterion Theater around the corner on Main Street, but I remember vividly what we saw as we came out of the theater.

In the early winter dusk people were still downtown, walking briskly along the street. Many were servicemen, already mobilized, perhaps stationed at Fort Sill in Lawton and were in the city on a weekend pass. Every one of them had a folded newspaper under his arm and a grim, purposeful look on his face.

A newsboy on the corner of Main and Broadway in corduroy knickers, zippered jacket, and six-penny cap, shouted, "*Extra, extra!*" It was as though a clip from a Hollywood movie had come alive. Dad bought a paper. The headlines were in type the size I would only see three times in my life: on December 7, 1941, and on the occasions of the end of the wars in Europe and the Pacific. As we walked back to our car, Dad read aloud. Pearl Harbor had been bombed by the Japanese, thereby sinking most of the U.S. Navy fleet, including the USS Oklahoma, which went down while most of its crew were still sleeping. War had begun in earnest and with heavy loss of life.

My overwhelming reaction was fear. "Will they bomb us?" I asked. The answer was reminiscent of the one I received about the picture of the child on the steps in Nanking. "No, it's too far away." However, I think I could sense the fear. If the Japanese could bomb Hawaii, they probably could bomb the West Coast. In truth, they attempted to send lighter-than-air craft to bring explosives to the US mainland. Troops stationed in the Aleutian Islands during the war were the troops closest to action on US soil. In addition, German U-boats patrolled deep into US coastal waters. Children my age would recall the blackout curtains on the windows of their homes for the duration of the war.

Within days of the attack on Pearl Harbor, I had my first personal experience with the far-off war. Before the war, the "Made in Japan" label appeared on cheap goods that were poorly made. From Japan we imported trinkets, toys, novelties, and downscale household items. The Japanese also made beautifully crafted small ornaments and accessories for dollhouses. I had a nice collection of doll furniture, which my family added to on birthdays and on Christmas.

On First Street in downtown Oklahoma City, just across the alley from the Skirvin Tower Hotel, a Japanese couple had a small shop that specialized in this merchandise along with other gift items. Shortly after the Pearl Harbor bombing, I was downtown with my mother, and we walked down to see what was in the shop. Long strips of paper tape held the broken windows precariously in place. The store was empty and stripped of all of its furnishings. I asked mother why the windows were broken and where the old couple had gone. She only shook her head and said, "I don't know." Later I wondered if the old couple had been sent to an internment camp. The matter was discussed at home in the context of one of my brother's high school friends of Japanese descent and the son of a truck farmer. The family was allowed to stay in Oklahoma because what they did was considered important for the "war effort." I never knew if there were other exceptions like this.

The constant in my life during the war years was school. The daily routine did not vary from the first Tuesday after Labor Day until the Friday before the Memorial Day weekend. We had breaks only at Thanksgiving, Christmas, and Easter. We spent our summer vacations in northern Wisconsin where my parents had built a house during the winter of 1941–1942. They chose a location on a lovely lake near the tiny village of Hazelhurst.

The war instantly made a difference in some obvious ways. Petroleum was vital to the war effort. Exploration and drilling went along at a frantic pace. For consumers there was gasoline rationing, perhaps the most obvious intrusion of the war into the lives of ordinary citizens. The government moved quickly to set up all sorts of operations for an all-out war that affected both civilians and the military. Large items such as automobiles were not manufactured for civilian use. The war touched everyone and everything.

The Cadillac my parents purchased in 1939 carried us everywhere throughout the war, and my mother drove it until 1952. It needed only minor repairs or replacement of water pumps, belts, and tires whenever they could be purchased. After the war, she had it repainted, replacing the original soft brown paint with glossy black and a bright red stripe below the glass. The original tan leather seats were recovered with red and blue plaid, bound in red leatherette. The effect was described by one of my junior-high friends as making it look like a real gangster's car.

We managed to save enough gas-ration stamps to drive to Wisconsin in 1942, our first summer in the house. It had absolutely no furniture except for the old army cots on which we slept. Mother made a foray to Hildebrand's Furniture Store in Rhinelander, Wisconsin, the county seat of Oneida County and its largest community. First, she asked to buy appliances, including a stove and a refrigerator. "Lady," the salesman began, "Don't you know there's a war on? I can't sell you those things. They're frozen."

"But you have them," she countered, "They're right there in the showroom."

"We can't sell them. We'll get arrested and fined."

"But I have a new house and no appliances."

He looked incredulous. "You mean you have nothing to cook on?"

"Not even a wood stove."

"Then you are the only person I know I can sell appliances to."

He confirmed that the new house had been under roof by December 7. Those were the guidelines of the Office of Price Administration (OPA). One of President Roosevelt's actions after Pearl Harbor was to establish the OPA to prevent profiteering during the war. This included the price of crude oil, which was $1.21 per barrel. Mother bought the stove and refrigerator, and both had huge round OPA stickers on them. She then proceeded to buy most of the rest of the furniture for the house.

Chapter 5

THE DURATION

ALTHOUGH OUR LIVES did not change in routine, the war pervaded everything we did, and everything we thought. Meat, shoes, sugar, tires, and gasoline were all strictly rationed. Mother carried her rationing stamps everywhere she went inside an oilcloth envelope I had made as a Campfire Girl project. Almost every student in grade school lined up in the library one day a week to buy a 25-cent savings stamp that we pasted into a book. When the book was full, we could trade it for a ten-year savings bond.

With gasoline rationing, we could not make the drive to Wisconsin's north woods each summer. Instead, we took the train. We had transportation when we arrived because my father and my brother Thurman drove from the station to the lake in the brown Chevrolet Uncle Charles left behind when he went overseas. We saved enough gasoline rationing stamps to get it there one way; in the winter it was kept at the local Mobil station.

During the wartime summers we rode the train north, taking the Santa Fe overnight to Chicago and the Milwaukee Road on to the little town of Hazelhurst near the lake. In addition to the excitement of its Pullman sleeping cars, the train was jammed with servicemen and women. They took every seat, and some spent the trip from Chicago north to their destination sitting on their luggage.

There seemed to be almost as many women as men in the service. The WACs in their starched khakis were impressive, but it was the Navy WAVEs in their summer whites with smart navy epaulettes and bands around their jaunty hats that fascinated me most. The chair cars we rode north from Chicago were noisy and smoky, but I contented myself with making up stories about the riders—where they came from and where they were going. I had no doubt that if I had been old enough, I would have followed those women into the ranks.

For the men, to be found 4-F and unfit for service was humiliating. My Uncle Karl, married to my mother's youngest sister Virginia, tried repeatedly to join the Navy but was turned down because of a knee he had injured playing football. Just before his Army draft number was to come up, the Navy finally took him. He was an employee of the Eastman Kodak Company, and the Navy decided they needed his film and photography expertise. He spent a particularly nasty war in the jungles of the Philippines developing and printing films of the war's battles and atrocities. After the war, one of my cousins showed me a photo of a severed Japanese head in a sling.

Uncle Karl sent me a pair of Navy denim dungarees, my first blue jeans. I wore them proudly with an old white dress shirt of my father's and a white cotton Navy "gob's" cap I had acquired somewhere. One summer, a stop in Chicago afforded me my first real look at a major city. My father took Thurman and me to the Rosenwald Museum of Science and Industry. I remember Dad's enthusiasm. He especially loved the exhibit that depicted aspects of the oil business, and he explained to us how the rotary, diamond, and core bits were used. He also took us to ride the "el" (the elevated train) all the way to the end of the line. I have no idea what direction we went, but for years afterwards I had nightmares in which blocks of dreary rowhouses appeared with wash hanging on lines behind them. The dull red of the brick was made even dingier by the coal dust that gave the air a bitter smell. The terrible drab sameness terrified me. There was nothing safe or imaginative there as I saw it. Something in the scene inspired suspicion and horror in me. I could not conceive how anyone could live in such crowded and mean circumstances without being damaged by it. The picture returns to me in some subliminal form each time I read about, meet, or hear of someone who became prominent after coming from such a background. I had no idea that for millions this was simply called home.

Our winter routine was dominated by thoughts of the war. Mother took down a colorful string of painted Mexican gourds and replaced it with a map of Europe and the Mediterranean area mounted on a piece of beaverboard. The map came from the *National Geographic* and was painstakingly detailed. I suppose if my Uncle Charles had been in the Pacific theater of war, Mother would have mounted a map of the Pacific Rim. As it was, the personal strains of the conflict manifested in strange ways. Everyone was prone to answer even a slightly unreasonable request with the riposte "Don't you know there's a war on?" My Aunt Virginia returned to Oklahoma City with her two small sons to wait out the war near her family while her husband was in the South Pacific. She and my mother engaged in a subtle rivalry. The argument always turned on whether the European or the Pacific wars were the worst and which of the men was in greater danger.

My Uncle Charles had married and had fathered a son before he was sent to England. He left my mother in charge of all his finances. As with so many wartime marriages, the couple did not really know each other, and he found he mistrusted his wife's ability to handle money. Since mother held the purse strings, except for the Army check that was sent directly to my uncle's wife, this did not endear the sisters-in-law to each other. But for the most part, people tried to maintain a façade of civility, keeping in mind the much larger sacrifices endured by the men and women in the armed forces.

War news was the topic of the day. With the shortage of newsprint, the publishers ceased printing the afternoon *Oklahoma City Times*. It would not resume publication until the war ended. But the morning paper was read avidly. The paper always included a map that depicted military activity. We became familiar with such North African names as El Alamein, Dakar, and Tunisia. On the second or third page of every edition, the paper listed the dead, missing, and wounded who were from Oklahoma, often with photos. There were stories of Oklahoma servicemen and women and accounts of their deeds derived from interviews or correspondence.

News of the war on the radio gave us a sense of immediacy. I remember lying in bed with the measles and listening to the live radio report of the fall of Tunis to the Allies. The last year of my grandfather's life was dominated by the hourly news broadcasts. It was the only time I heard my grandmother complain—in the kitchen and out of his hearing, of course. The constant repetition, with only slight differences in each retelling, drove her mad. It was a precursor of more egregious things to come, such as CNN's twenty-four-hour coverage of any "breaking news"—real, rumored, or trivial.

The war years had their lighter moments. In addition to the war news on the radio was the entertainment that we loved. We used our imaginations to fill in the visual gaps.

We especially loved the Sunday-evening radio shows that included Edgar Bergen and Charlie McCarthy, Fred Allen, George Burns and Gracie Allen, the Quiz Kids, and the intellectual roundtable of Clifton Fadiman, Oscar Levant, and Franklin P. Adams on *Information Please*. The characters on *One Man's Family* were as familiar to us as the members of our own family. Every day after school, Thurman and I loved to listen to *Jack Armstrong, The Lone Ranger* and *Captain Midnight* in the afternoon. Evenings were filled with *Inner Sanctum, I Love a Mystery, Lux Radio Theater,* and the humor of Art Linkletter.

Saturday's shows were my favorites. I didn't outgrow listening to *Let's Pretend* until I went to junior high school. The winter afternoons brought the Texaco-sponsored Metropolitan Opera performances. These performances and my mother's taking me to symphony concerts led to a life-long love of classical music. I was devastated when there were no opera performances during the summer. The radio also brought us nonsense songs like "Three Little Fishies" and "Mairzy Doats" along with the sounds of Glenn Miller, the Dorseys, and Artie Shaw. It was from radio broadcasts that I learned all the words to the songs from *Oklahoma!* Later my family and I attended its first performance in Oklahoma City in 1943 with both Rodgers and Hammerstein in the audience. Radio and movie personalities turned their talents to the war effort, not just to entertain the men and women in the service but to raise money. A highlight for me was listening to Red Skelton and later to Edgar Bergen with all his puppets and the entire crew of his radio show at a bond rally in the Municipal Auditorium. I discovered that Bergen moved his lips when Charlie talked.

One thing that stood out from the newspaper accounts that promoted the event was the announcement that there would be plenty of room set aside in the balcony for Black service personnel and their families. Jim Crow was alive and well despite the hostilities overseas.

The radio shows, like our daily lives, went on without much alteration. The soap operas, the radio comics, and the morning shows such as *The Breakfast Club* would transfer their familiar fare to *The Today Show* on television without much change in format. The actors in the soaps would acquire beautiful clothes, and *Information, Please* would metamorphose into *Jeopardy*.

And for me, there were always books. I read constantly, including boys' books like *Treasure Island* and *Robinson Crusoe* as well as *Little Women* and the Laura Ingalls Wilder series. From these I graduated into adult fiction with such classics as *Madame Bovary* as well as contemporary popular fiction. I read novels by James Hilton. By 1944, I was reading John Hersey's Pulitzer Prize-winning *A Bell for Adano,* as well as the scandalous (for those days) *Forever Amber*. Mention of that book always brings a smile to my face. One day in October of 1944, grandmother and I were riding the streetcar into town. She asked me if I could think of something to get my mother for her birthday and inquired if perhaps I knew of a new book she would like to read. "*Forever Amber,*" I whispered.

"What?" she said, and I was forced to say the title louder, hoping no one overheard me. She did buy it for my mother, who enjoyed it and let me read it. She said she thought the descriptions of the London plague and the fire were excellent. Obviously, the scenes with mildly explicit sex did not bother her. My brother introduced me to real pornography in Europe when I was sixteen, long after I had discovered Balzac, Restoration comedy, and Boccaccio. The days of war spun into months and years. We dealt with the routine of rationing, about which everyone grumbled and remarkably few cheated or profiteered from in any substantial way. For the most part, everyone gave what he or she could to the war effort. Mother took a Red Cross course and taught nutrition since everyone was dealing with rationing and scarcity. I suppose the Red Cross thought healthier children would make healthier future soldiers.

In 1942, after the tide of war turned in North Africa, the islands in the South Pacific were recaptured, and there were spectacular victories at sea, no one seriously doubted that the Allies would win, but the invasion of the mainland of Europe became our primary focus. The personalities of the World War II generals were as familiar to us as those of the Civil War generals were to the readers of *Lee's Lieutenants*. We knew about Patton's temper tantrums, Bradley's quiet leadership, Montgomery's swashbuckling, "Bulldog" Halsey's tenacity, and Eisenhower's leadership abilities.

MacArthur's egotism was well documented—the special uniform and the corncob pipe. His gift of leadership was shown in the South Pacific. No one knew the Far East better. No one could do a better job in Japan after the war. However, his extreme egotism later forced President Truman to fire him during the Korean War. Above all, we knew George Catlett Marshall stood at the helm.

For Oklahomans, the bloody and unromantic war in the Italian "boot" interested us most. The 45th Division, our National Guard division, bore the brunt of the fighting at Monte Casino. Here a cartoonist in that division, Bill Mauldin, made heroes out of the two "grunts" Willie and Joe. Mauldin's cartoons, first published in *Stars and_Stripes*, the US Army's newspaper, were soon carried by most dailies in the United States. If one goes back and reads the "Up Front" cartoons today, they bring back all the emotion of those days with their exquisite humor. Mauldin did for the European Theater what the journalist Ernie Pyle did for the Pacific. They made the war honest, personal, and timely and answered for millions of Americans the question "Have you seen my son/husband? What's it like, and how is he doing?"

Before television, radio and the newsreels kept us informed about the war and gave us a sense of immediacy. The black-and-white newsreels were like animations of the wire photos that were reproduced every day in newsprint. Even most of the pages of *LIFE* magazine were in black and white, but the sounds in the radio reports let us imagine the smoke, the blood, and the death. Newspaper coverage was incredibly good, given the strictures of necessarily managed news. Much of what we were fed was propaganda, but somehow we managed to sift out most of the real news from the government's spin. Edward R. Murrow was a voice of calm with his no-nonsense, direct reporting from overseas.

War news even invaded the classroom. *My Weekly Reader* was a national publication given to each student. Formatted like a small newspaper, the issues were simple for the early grades and more sophisticated for the higher grades. The news was covered in unusual depth for elementary-school children. I remember a series of articles that appeared near the end of the war that debated the merits and disadvantages of universal military training. Although later generations might have found the little newspaper boring, during the war it was full of real information packaged for children.

We discussed these articles in class, and we were particularly interested in the birth of the United Nations. My sixth-grade teacher Velma Herring made sure we knew about whatever was in *My Weekly Reader* as well as in the news for adults. Both Miss Herring and Ruth Patton, the other teacher of the upper two grades, had a great love of history. They particularly enjoyed teaching Oklahoma's Constitution and Oklahoma history. In the days before deconstruction, we were taught the facts and learned to study history without making value judgments. As with the bare bones reporting of the war news, the facts were more important than how we felt about them.

Although the overall curriculum did not change much, the war influenced everything we did after school. There were scrap-metal and paper drives. Boy Scouts collected newspapers, tin cans, and grease. Bacon grease was collected to make munitions, and the scrap metal was immediately recycled into war weapons. There was a shortage of paper, so newsprint was reclaimed to produce paper for record keeping and other needs. Long before the environmental movement arrived, conservation and waste management were in the forefront of everyone's mind. We never forgot the war for a moment. As a Blue Bird and a Campfire Girl, I knitted six-inch squares, which were gathered up and made into Afghans for the wounded.

Another unchangeable thing in our home was politics. My mother was a life-long Republican. Her opinion of Democrats was colored by the memory of her paternal grandfather, who was described by my grandmother as the only drunk and the only Democrat in Troutman, Pennsylvania. Despite mother's admiration for the characters in *The Grapes of Wrath*, she was a firm believer in "pulling yourself up by your own bootstraps," and "an honest day's work for an honest dollar." She hated Franklin Roosevelt. My father's opinion was more moderate. He voted for FDR in 1932. Neither of them approved of the public-works projects, but they admired the artwork and the new buildings that were subsidized, as well as the discipline of the Civilian Conservation Corps (CCC) camps. I had the impression that they admired the discipline of the camps because they thought the CCC was filled with incorrigible or lazy young men.

In 1940, I had two Willkie buttons; one was made of green celluloid and the other of pink. The buttons consisted of little bars with his name on them and a celluloid elephant hanging below. I thought them very clever, but mine were the only Willkie buttons in the class. The parents of my friends idolized FDR. Later, after Willkie lost the election to Roosevelt, the President asked the defeated candidate to become an ambassador at large. Willkie wrote the book *One World*, which I greatly admired, and I never regretted my non-voting support for the man. I was grieved at his early death. He stood for a new world order to me. As talk of *One World* increased, consensus grew among our allies that we should revive some sort of League of Nations to further the cooperation fostered by the war effort. I believed that only some super world confederation could solve the problem of war, so we would never again have to go through that kind of trauma.

Unlike the prevailing opinion in 1918, this time most US citizens were in favor of the experiment. Albert Einstein said in 1948, "There is only one path to peace and security: the path of supranational organization. One-sided armament on a national basis only heightens the general uncertainty and confusion without being an effective protection."

As early as second grade I began to be aware of the political divisions within my country. The elections of 1940 and 1944 taught me to stand my ground and taught me also about the breadth of the electorate. In the 1948 election, everyone, especially the *Chicago Tribune*, learned a lesson in caution. Predictions before the last ballot is counted can be dangerous to your credibility. The night the *Tribune* made its famous error, I went to bed confident that Thomas E. Dewey would be elected president. He was married to an Oklahoma native, a point of pride for me. To my surprise at breakfast, Truman was still president. It was almost as much of a shock as how he became president in the first place.

By the time of Roosevelt's last election, I was in the fifth grade. The fifth- and sixth-grade students were housed in the original red-brick school building. The old building, situated just behind the new one, had twelve-foot ceilings, huge Victorian windows with deep reveals, slate blackboards permanently streaked gray with chalk dust, musty restrooms in a half-basement, an almost derelict second floor, and fire escapes. We loved the fire escapes best. Instead of switchback stairs of open ironwork, they were enclosed silos with slides, turning two-and-a-half times around on their way from the second floor to the ground, which was a story-and-a-half lower. When the school fair was held to raise money for library books, we could pay a penny to slide all the way down on the magic carpet of a gunnysack.

The new building, with its yellow brick and art-deco embellishments, faced south and housed grades kindergarten through fourth, along with the cafeteria, the principal's office, the library, and an auditorium that was hung in red velvet. Now the old building was gone; the heavy iron escapes were carted away for scrap, and the wide planks were burned, probably still smelling of oil and of the cedar shavings from the pencil sharpeners scattered by the custodian with his wide broom as he cleaned the floor. When the building was demolished, workmen cleaned and stacked the bricks in rows. They were sold to give an old look to new houses. Many of them were used in building the home my husband's parents built. I wonder if some satellite with an infrared eye can see the square-cornered outline where the foundation of the school used to be?

Along with December 7, 1941, D-Day, June 6, 1944, was an unforgettable day. The landing of troops in Europe was keenly anticipated. We were at our summer house in Wisconsin in June of 1944. My brother Thurman invited his friend Joe to join us that summer. Joe always wore a Navy seaman's hat, a gift from his father who had been in a Japanese prison camp after the fall of Bataan. That day in June, Joe came bounding up the stairs of the summer house, his eyes wide, to announce that the Normandy landing had begun.

April 12, 1945, was also a memorable day. It began with a momentous series of events and an astounding climax to the long war. On that day, my best friend Wanda Young and I watched all day long as clouds piled in the northwest, purple and ugly as a bruise—tornado weather. During afternoon recess, we watched the fourth-grade girls playing jacks while we kept what Grandmother called a "weather eye" on the clouds. At the same moment, in Warm Springs, Georgia, the only man to be President of the United States in our lifetime slumped over in his wheelchair and died as he was sitting for his portrait. The portrait remained unfinished.

After recess, my mother called the school to tell me not to come home; she would pick me up because of the coming storm. She was late, unusual for her. I stood alone in the old building, looking out a window at the sky that was black; above it was a rolling cloud with a strip of brilliant, colorless sky below. The slanting light turned the grass chartreuse. Maples turned up the silver side of their leaves like shining five-fingered hands to ward off the storm.

I had ridden my blue Hawthorn bicycle to school, so when she arrived, my mother said, "Let's get your bike inside out of the weather." We bumped the bicycle down the basement stairs and locked it next to the girls' restroom and then quickly escaped the smell of mildew and Lysol. There was no wind, but the underside of the cloud had begun to boil. As we dashed for our brown Cadillac parked near the opening in the chain-link fence, the first huge drops of rain spattered my plaid dress, saddle shoes, and socks. I put my notebook on my head to avoid having to roll and dry my recently permanent-waved hair. By the time we reached the car we were thoroughly soaked.

Mother leaned across the seat and unlocked the door for me, holding it against the rising wind. When I was safely inside, she maneuvered the car through side winds and sudden torrents of rain. Concentrating on the windshield that was barely cleared by the wipers, she remarked, "Oh, by the way, did you hear? President Roosevelt died this afternoon." Perhaps her matter-of-fact tone was due to her preoccupation with guiding the car through the storm, or maybe it was because her life-long Republicanism kept her from any sense of regret for FDR's demise. I did not inquire but sat stunned by the news. In those moments of silence, the fat finger of a tornado reached down close to the Canadian River, too far away to harm us but on-target to kill more than sixty citizens and to devastate the poorest part of Oklahoma City. The same storm system rolled on to obliterate most of the town of Antlers.

Mother finally parked the car in the garage. I hurried to my room to listen to the news on the radio and learned about the obscure vice president named Harry Truman who was now my president. I wondered if a dead commander-in-chief would merit a gold star in the window of the White House. Victory was supposed to be like the movies, happy and free of surprises. But in Eastern Europe, the first scant reports of the fate of others who wore gold stars—stars of David—became known to us. Within the next three weeks, the world would see for the first time the naked, dead, and nearly fleshless bodies of the survivors of the Holocaust, clad in dirty striped rags of prison uniforms. Reports of the gas showers and ovens were vivid enough even in the black-and-white of newspapers and their grainy wire photos to evoke the stench of burning flesh half a world away. Photographs of stacks of eyeglasses and a mountain of mismatched shoes lent credibility to the unbelievable display. Woody Guthrie wrote a song about a female member of the Gestapo who made lampshades of human skin, a widely circulated story at the time that was never verified.

Our side hid its own surprises. Somewhere in Los Alamos, New Mexico, final plans were made to detonate a new weapon on the sandy plains of that state. Scientists preparing did not know whether setting off the test bomb would start a chain reaction that would blow the world apart. Early in June they would be relieved when all that appeared after the blast was sand crystallized to glass and a peculiar cloud that was of their own making. Scientists didn't know much about the radiation in the cloud that made it even more deadly than the cloud that brought tornadoes.

By April we knew the war would soon be over. I secretly hoped that the final surrender of Nazi Germany would occur on my twelfth birthday. All winter, my brother and I moved pins on a map on the wall of the breakfast room, watching the pregnant bulge of the Third Reich's last great counterattack swell into Belgium and finally collapse when confronted by clearing weather and the arrival of Patton's Third Army to the rescue of the 101st Airborne Division. They came by tank rather than horses, but they seemed to us like the cavalry in the movies we saw at the Ritz Theater on Saturdays. The tanks got the glory, but it was the half-frozen GIs on the ground who stopped the enemy's advance.

There was still more death, none of it caused by a natural disaster or old age and illness. On an island called Okinawa, another of the bloody campaigns for the Pacific was being carried out. This would be the last island-based campaign. It lasted for ninety days until the middle of June and added thousands of gold stars to the galaxies that were hanging in the windows of many American families. They had blue stars for those who had served their country and gold stars for those who had died for it. On the same island, American troops used flame-throwers to flush out the enemy. Japanese soldiers ran from caves as their bodies became living torches and their limbs looked like charred bacon. Japanese casualties would exceed 86,000 men, and American losses would almost equal the 22,000 that fell at Iwo Jima. In addition, island citizens were killed in the battle, most of them Japanese. The names on the monument dedicated fifty years later, number 234,183. The following August, the bombings in Hiroshima and Nagasaki would produce grainy photographs of white shadows on concrete where bodies had vaporized and young Japanese girls had shreds of skin peeling from radiation burns.

But on April 12, all I wanted was the safety of home. I couldn't know that after 1945, the world would never be the same. With the war nearly won, I let myself believe the words of a popular song about "bluebirds over the white cliffs of Dover." I let myself believe fascism was finally defeated, dead and buried, and that there had been too much blood and sacrifice for it ever to rise again. By September, when the unconditional surrender of Japan was signed aboard the USS Missouri, my world had become completely reoriented.

Chapter 6

SCHOOL DAYS

BY SEPTEMBER 1945, I was enrolled in Harding Junior High School and would go on to Classen High School where the children from Northwest Oklahoma City went to school. Mother wanted me to go to the public high school, which was considered to be the best for college preparation. Her reasons, however, were as much social as academic. I could have gone to either Central High School or Northeast, the new high school Thurman attended, but Mother insisted that I go to Harding and Classen. The message her decision sent was clear; girls had to be socially acceptable. This had something to do with sororities and being marriageable.

I remember the yellow linen dress that I wore the first day at Harding. It was the prettiest dress I had ever owned; somehow, I knew the importance of looking good and fitting in. I was terrified but survived the day despite changing classes each hour, all the unfamiliar faces, and the new teachers. On days my mother could not drive me to school, I rode public transportation because there were no school buses in the city. The experience was instructive. I rode the bus in the morning with the mostly Black passengers, including women on their way to domestic work across town, and back home in the afternoon with many of the same people. We did not speak.

"Remember," my mother instructed me, "if there is no room in the white section, you may sit in the colored section, but then if a colored person gets on, you should give them your seat." I was puzzled by the rules. I am not sure if mother made up her own rules, but they seemed reasonable, if curious, to a child reared in segregation. I took this lesson in bus etiquette seriously but never had to face the problem. The metal signs read "colored" on one side and "white" on the other and were hung at a ninety-degree angle to the aisle. They were mounted on a pivot, so the only thing the bus driver had to do was turn the sign to indicate whether more of the seats were reserved for blacks or whites.

By my second year at school, a carpool formed to drive the few children from our side of town who attended Harding and Classen Senior High. Often, instead of a parent, an older brother of one of the girls would take us to Harding and go on to Classen. I soon became aware that all of us "eastsiders" were treated with condescension, as though we lived across the Santa Fe tracks because our parents could not afford to live on the west side. The difference was subtle, but by the time I was in high school, this attitude would become explicit.

The only person I knew at Harding was Phyllis Cooper. At one time her family lived a block away, and our mothers became friends. Phyllis remained my closest friend for ninety years. We were fortunate to forge one of those friendships that endured time and separation. We never lived in the same town after college. "They've been friends since diapers," my mother would sometimes comment to people.

Phyllis and I were asked to join the Happy Hearts Club, a junior high sorority. I was now part of an elite, but something about the exclusivity made me uncomfortable. I knew my former grade-school friends would not be welcome here among the children of privilege. One spring my mother held a party for me in the back yard of our house on Sixteenth Street. Not only did the parents have to transport their daughters across the tracks to get to our neighborhood, but some of the local boys threw dirt over the brick wall in an effort to get the girls' attention or to show contempt or both. Some of the dirt clods ended up on the girls' plates, and my mother was mortified.

Mother and Dad joined the Beacon Club downtown, and any further entertaining I did through junior and senior high was done there. Clubs and organizations were important among my mother's friends and their daughters. High school taught me some hard lessons in social behavior; I was not asked to join a high-school sorority. I suppose I still hold the record for being blackballed more times than any other girl in the history of the institution. My friends, bless them, kept proposing me for membership right up to our senior year.

These organizations held subtle power in my school. Even if you had excellent grades, which I did, you were never elected to any office associated with the school unless you belonged to a sorority. What I did instead was turn my leadership abilities to organizations outside the school where I could exert some influence and learned to be adaptable and flexible. I was president of the young girl's organization at our Episcopal church and of the Junior Lady's Music Club.

My good grades also provided a cover for other activities. When I was sixteen, my parents bought me a car to make the trip across town to school. I was one of the few students to have a car of her own, although many of my classmates drove the family automobile occasionally to school, sometimes giving friends a ride. The car gave me freedom, and I began to hang out with the guys. By the time I was a senior,

I logged many hours in all the beer joints where students knew that being underage was not a problem.

I was introduced to a new boy from Fort Worth named Henry B. "Boots" Taliaferro, Jr. Boots transferred to Harding in the eighth grade, and by the time he was in the ninth grade he was elected student-council president by a single vote. I was impressed; Boots had that elusive quality called charisma. Although I dated other boys, I found myself following Boots's career with special interest, including the girls he dated. He was aware of me mostly as the daughter of friends of his parents. When he went to college at the University of Oklahoma, I had my father drive me to Norman to the Kappa Sigma House where my brother lived. Boots's father as well as mine had been members of that fraternity. However, I was not surprised when Boots joined another fraternity along with a group of his high-school friends.

But boys were not my only interest; I continued to love school, and learning. The summer of 1949 brought with it another seminal experience. Mother and her best friend from California, whom we called Aunt Lynn, took Thurman and me to Europe. We traveled for nearly four months, from the last week in May until after the first week in September. We crossed the Atlantic on the old Cunard liner the Mauritania. It was truly a grand tour; we visited France, Italy, Switzerland, Holland, Belgium, England, Scotland, and Wales.

My first glimpse of the Champs Elysée and the Arc de Triomphe made a huge impression on me. "They're real," I said to myself. "Picture postcards come to life." The paintings and buildings that my mother had shown me pictures of in books were exponentially more impressive in person. Walking through the Dahlem district in Berlin, the Tate Gallery in London, or the Uffizi Gallery in Florence can still reduce me to tears.

There were vivid reminders of war everywhere. All the French railroad stations were being reconstructed. Naples was rebuilding. We spent our time in Germany with friends of my mother who were with the American military government. Only four years after its defeat, Germany was an occupied nation. We saw few older men, and many of the younger ones had the lost limbs and scars of battle. In one Bavarian church we watched a wedding; the bride was in her twenties and the groom was at least sixty.

Munich and Nuremberg were completely destroyed. But Germany, unlike France, had already rebuilt its railroad stations. Driving through the city of Munich was unforgettable. You would see a building from a distance and think perhaps it had not been touched, only to approach and find that it, too, was a shell. There was rubble in every direction. Our host's daughter had been in the United States all winter in college but was home with her family while we visited. We thought the devastation was unthinkable, but her comment was, "But it's so cleaned up."

Just as surprising to us were the views of our guide in Avignon, a young man who had been in the French resistance. He was a dedicated communist. He and my mother spent hours arguing and discussing politics as we sat in a grape arbor in the evening.

Britain was in the throes of austerity. The Labor government was determined to dig out from the war debt, and as a consequence its population had been deprived of everything but necessities during the war and was still queuing up for the few goods that were available. Tons of rabbits were shipped in from Australia. I remember having few meals with meat except for some roast beef at Simpson's restaurant on the Strand in London.

The National Health Service (NHS) was just beginning, and although health care was universally available, the vagaries of the new system became a popular topic among the British at the time. They grumbled about the sterility and uniformity of the system. My eyeglasses, with their bright blue aluminum frames, were a particular curiosity to people. Nothing like them was available anywhere in England through the NHS.

Thurman returned to the States by air from London, ostensibly to be on time for the start of his junior year at the university. In truth, he flew back because he was in a hurry to see Marilyn Bemis, whom he would marry the following spring. Mother, Aunt Lynn, and I sailed back on the Parthia, a smaller, more intimate ship than the Mauritania.

I learned the joys of drinking table wine in Europe. Mother saw no reason for me not to drink the wine since she was unsure of the quality of the water in many places. On shipboard I met a young Canadian who introduced me to Capstan cigarettes and the art of the French kiss. I also had a firsthand lesson in economics. When we left England, the pound was worth five US dollars. When we were halfway across the Atlantic news came over the radio that the British government had devalued the pound to $2.50. This meant any British subject who left Southampton with the equivalent of a thousand dollars to last for the duration of the trip abroad would arrive in New York with only five hundred dollars. I particularly remember one young man who was desperately challenging anyone on the ship to a game of ping-pong, hoping to win enough to cope with the shortfall in his carefully planned budget.

In August, two momentous things happened to upset the balance of political power in the world. First, Russia exploded its first nuclear device; it now had the atom bomb. And Mao Tse Tung finally completed his revolution in China; it was now a communist country. No matter how vivid our lessons and impressions during our travels were, the transforming experiences of the 1940s had to do with the recent war and its consequences. People who had lived through the war would spend much of their lifetime viewing the world through the prism of a ridiculously short time period—April through August of 1945.

More than fifty years later, Lincoln School has become the High School of Math and Science and no longer teaches grade schoolers. The spring winds still push at the hard red clay near what we called the New Building. The auditorium, little changed, is still hung in red velvet. In 1998 I watched as high-school students gathered at the front of that same auditorium to question a speaker about the newest advances in genetics. Their young faces were crowded out by my memories of five- and six-pointed stars, strange clouds, tornadoes, burning enemy soldiers, and striped prison uniforms. Other images crowded in, like those that appeared on the stark black-and-white pages of *LIFE* magazine —pictures of a black Sergeant at President Roosevelt's funeral playing the accordion as tears streaked down his cheeks. They showed dead Marines on beaches; naked skeletons by the thousands, and two mushroom clouds— one over Nagasaki and another over Hiroshima. Images carefully folded into the shape of the origami cranes and hung on threads of memory, the way paper cranes decorate the shrine at Hiroshima.

The summer before I left for college, two events changed my life. My father, born in the Victorian era, had his personal view of women. He truly placed them on a pedestal. He was constantly giving me advice about being ladylike and often quoted the Bible and Shakespeare, although he was neither religious nor much of a reader except of science. He would admonish me to keep my voice low and soothing. Once, when I was about sixteen, he gave me a book about love that offered an overly romantic and idealistic treatment.

Regardless of this attitude, he did an astonishing thing, something he had not done for my brother. In the summer of 1951, he took me to his office and wrote a check for $4,000. This was enough money in those days to pay for my four years of tuition, for my books, and for board and room at the dormitory and later the sorority house where I would eventually live after my freshman year.

He handed it to me with a statement and a question. The statement was, "This is your college money. If you run out, you go to work." His question was, "Now, what are you going to do with it?"

"Put it in the bank?"

"How much money will you make in interest?" he asked.

I replied, stating the minuscule amount the banks were paying at the time.

"Can you think of something else to do with it?"

I thought a moment and asked about the Fenner and Beane place he was always talking about. I knew nothing about the stock market.

He nodded and walked me down the street to the bank and the brokerage house. First, we opened a bank account with the money and ordered checks for me. At the time, he was cosigner on the account because women then were not allowed to open bank accounts in their own names. After that we went to Merrill Lynch and talked about what would happen there. I opted to invest $3,000 of the $4,000 in common stock.

My father taught me how to read Standard and Poor's ratings. I invested in blue-chip stocks, beginning with US Steel. I remember its symbol at the time was simply "X." Later I bought American Express primarily because I read it had paid dividends all through the Depression. My sorority sisters teased me about my tracking my money every day in the paper, but I did not care. I paid for my college education and had enough left to buy clothes. Finally, when I graduated, I still had $4,000 in the bank. I had doubled my money, and I eventually used it as part of a down payment on the first house my husband and I bought. I must quickly add what students of the US stock market will recognize; I had caught the first great bull market of the post-war period; I couldn't lose.

None of this good fortune was due to my intelligence and perspicacity. It was pure luck, and I was smart enough to recognize it. But I learned the lessons. I knew about financial cycles, and I knew about how much control one might or might not have over financial affairs. I learned to budget and to save. My father's words were precious to me. "The pace of business is very slow," he would say. "Don't get in a hurry and let your emotions dictate what you do." He cautioned me about getting into the operating side of the oil and gas business and said he always regretted not buying more commercial real estate.

All this advice would come back to me thirty years later when I would make some of the mistakes that he warned me about. I would then take his advice to heart and be guided by the lessons I had learned when I was dealing in millions rather than thousands. What I learned from Dad about handling would be of value to me for years to come. However, something else happened that summer that would influence my later efforts on behalf of women's rights; I was the victim of sexual assault.

It was a classic instance of date rape. I had gone out with this young man once before, and on our first date I was put off by his aggressive behavior. We had not been drinking, an unusual thing for me. I think I accepted the dates because he was a major-league athlete and I was flattered. At the end of an unremarkable evening, he drove to one of the more popular places to park in Oklahoma City. His attack was quick and forceful. In those days, automobiles had bench seats. I found myself on my back; terrified, I began to scream, my voice sounding to my own ears like bleating. My first thought was that I was going to die; rape and murder were inexorably linked in my mind.

The reality that rape is not an act of sex but one of violence does not seem to register with young men, but for young women it is an entirely different matter. To be so completely under the physical power of another person is a terrible reminder of how helpless one can be. Afterward I was beset by all the emotions typically felt by women. It was my fault; I should not have been with him. Did the care with which I dressed for the evening have anything to do with what happened?

Just as vivid as the memory of the attack was what happened when I got home. I went to the bathroom and was appalled when I felt semen running out of my body. I do not know if it was due to fear or if I was actually pregnant, but I missed a menstrual period after the assault took place. I was overwhelmed by an enormous, helpless fear.

The circumstances were so very different in 1951 than today. I absolutely could not talk to my parents about it because I felt so ashamed. I had no doctor or priest with whom I felt comfortable enough to discuss the matter. Even if I had done so, in those days they would have known better than to recommend that I do anything other than go to a home for unwed mothers. Retreating to such homes and putting babies up for adoption were considered the only alternative. Legal abortions were done rarely and only under the most extreme circumstances for medical reasons. They were typically performed only on married women. Any self-respecting doctor or priest knew better than to suggest abortion. My only course of action would have led to the back alley and possibly to sterilization or death. This was truly the day of the coat hanger.

I could not face either hiding a pregnancy or giving up a child. My solution would have been suicide. I now know that at the time I suffered from depression, which was not unusual in late adolescence. My solution to an unwanted pregnancy was simple: suicide. I did not recognize it at the time, but I was also suffering from adolescent depression. Years before the Me Too movement, I would relate the entire story at a Planned Parenthood dinner given in my honor. I wanted everyone to know the importance of all the services provided by the agency, from prevention to education, and, if needed, termination. Fortunately, I didn't have to make the decision. My period finally appeared, late. Instead of the grave, I put all this behind me in some mental closet, packed my car, and went to Dallas and Southern Methodist University (SMU).

Chapter 7

UNIVERSITY

THE THREE AND a half years I spent at Southern Methodist University in Dallas were full—too full—of activity. For some reason I was in a tearful hurry to finish college and had no clear idea of what I would do after graduation. My vague goal was to continue with a master's degree and teach college-level English. I had no desire to teach at a lower level and was probably more motivated by a love of academia than any sort of career commitment.

The ostensible reasons for my choosing to attend nearby SMU rather than going away to college were my mother's illness and my brother's posting to Korea. But the real reason was fear. In my senior high-school year I gave up the idea of attending Vassar, my first choice. I didn't want to take the college boards. Regardless of my good grade average, I was afraid I wouldn't do well. Instead, I chose the school closer to home that did not have such stringent entrance requirements. Such fears did not deter my dearest friend, Phyllis Cooper. She took the boards and went to Smith for two years until the death of her father forced her to return to Oklahoma to finish her degree.

As I look back, I realize that some teachers and courses in college were profoundly life changing, even though I could not see it at the time. It was one long round of classes, winter and summer. As much as I loved school and still do, it was hard for me to think of myself as a scholar. In my senior year, Dr. Gusta Barfield Nance called me into her office and offered me the chance to graduate with honors. I had no idea what graduating with honors really meant, I only knew it would necessitate writing one more paper, and I declined.

"You know," I said, "I am not really a scholar." She looked at me with disbelief but did not argue. Finally, she said my grades were such that I would at least graduate with departmental honors. I left her office with no sense of having given up anything other than the hours it would take to write the paper.

Grades had ceased to be a major concern to me after the second semester of my freshman year when I made a "B" in World Civilization. The grade precluded me from joining the freshman honorary society, and it eventually pulled my average down just enough to miss Phi Beta Kappa. Somehow in my mind this translated to a lack of intellectual dedication or ability. Along the way, several courses changed my outlook on the world. The first was a year of Greek.

As a freshman I took two semesters of classic Greek in lieu of one semester of algebra. I was terrified of taking any mathematics. The result was not one I expected. Studying Greek reinforced my love of classic literature, and I found the etymology a fascinating window into the way the ancient Greeks thought. Their intuitive knowledge about the inner workings of the human mind riveted me. The course in classical Greek led to my majoring in comparative literature, the department headed by Dr. Nance. I had most of my major's serious work under her. Here I had my first brush with a famous person. At the beginning of class each day, I knew Dr. Nance would call either on me or on Mrs. Mansfield, who sat in the front row. I always hid in the back row, with a bottle of Coca-Cola—which on at least one occasion I spilled—under my chair. In addition, I had the habit of working on the crossword puzzle in the campus newspaper each day in class. Nevertheless, I was always prepared, and Dr. Nance knew it.

Mrs. Mansfield was also always prepared. I admired her. She was already married, and I believe a mother, even though she was just my age. Still, she pursued her college career with diligence. It was unusual in the extreme to find a young married woman in class, although many of the World War II veterans were married when they went to college, and their wives sometimes attended classes. By the time I went to SMU most of those students had graduated. Mrs. Mansfield was about my size and very quiet. She was always neatly dressed, and her medium brown hair was a little more than shoulder length. She was an excellent student. Years later I would have to go back to the college yearbook to confirm that the flamboyant blonde actress with the heart-shaped swimming pool, Jayne Mansfield, was indeed the same person.

I felt an almost personal loss at her tragic death in an automobile accident in Louisiana. I was struck by the stark difference between her public and private persona. The public one was made of celluloid and cardboard. The real woman was a fascinating contrast. I would never again completely trust what I read about a person, no matter how in-depth the biography is.

I received an introduction to the power of the press in another way. Our campus newspaper, appropriately named *The Campus*, went on a crusade protesting a book written by an extremely right-wing professor. I do not remember the exact circumstances of how the controversy arose. Perhaps the author was invited to speak at SMU or one of our history professors used the book in his class. Whatever the cause, the university's newspaper considered the book pro-fascist and went after the author with undergraduate zeal. The discussion was spirited, but I found myself coming down on the side of the First Amendment. The man was a distinguished professor, and in my opinion, he had a right to say what he wanted. The controversy finally died down when enough voices raised concerns about freedom of speech and the First Amendment.

These years were also my introduction to a different, more insidious power—the power of selective journalistic focus. The Korean War began the year before I went to college, and the hostilities did not end until the summer of 1953, just before my junior year. During those last years of the war, I read the *Dallas Morning News* every day. My brother and many of my friends were in Korea. I was irritated every day when I had to search the paper, often deeply in the second section, to find any news of the war. The entire experience was so different from that of World War II less than five years before, when the war often seemed to be the only news.

If I was preoccupied by Korea, I was also aware of other changes in society. *Brown v. Board of Education* was decided by the Supreme Court in 1954. I vaguely thought of joining the lunch-counter sit-ins, but I wasn't close enough to the protests to consider it seriously. When SMU admitted the first Black student to its theology school, I cheered the action and followed the controversies over school integration. It was the first time I heard the name George Wallace.

For me, the 1950s are divided into *before* and *after* the Army-McCarthy hearings. *Before* was my senior year in high school and the move with my parents to the exclusive part of town, followed by nearly four years of college. *After* the hearings came graduation, marriage, the birth of two of my three children, and participating in my first political campaign. By the time I went to college, television sets were beginning to show up in most private homes. We had a lounge area inside my sorority house where the huge black box of a television was the most prominent feature. We all gathered in the evening to sit on the floor and watch television. There were so few TV channels, mostly only the three networks, but I do not recall any disagreement over what we would watch. Being college women, we did our share of watching the news.

World War II had been a radio and newsreel war, while the Korean War was mostly reported in the newspapers. The Army-McCarthy hearings were the first great public television event. The hearings and the nominating conventions of the two parties were new occasions for us to watch what was going on in Washington. Although my political leanings were still influenced by my parents, both strong Republicans, the hearings caused my first political and philosophical rift with my family. I often went home to Oklahoma City during my college years, more than I actually wanted to. By 1951, my mother was suffering the first stages of the severe rheumatoid arthritis that would keep her mostly confined to a wheelchair from 1954 until 1960 and bedridden from then until her death in 1965.

When I was home, my mother and I watched the hearings together. She had nothing but contempt for Democrats, but it was difficult for her to keep the faith with Republican Senator Joseph McCarthy as the party's spokesperson. In addition, she greatly admired the skill of Joseph Welch, the lead counsel for the Army's investigation of McCarthy. I had no trouble selecting my side of the argument; I thought McCarthy was abhorrent. Something of the zealot about him repelled me. His accusations seemed theatrical and his evidence suspect.

Another rift in my rock-ribbed Republican background appeared during the first Eisenhower-Stevenson presidential election. Still not twenty-one, which was the voting age in those days, I could not cast a vote for president in 1952, despite being an admirer and supporter of Eisenhower. During this time, I was taking a class called the History of American Ideas. My best friend in college, Carolyn Collier, was a history major, and she insisted I attend this class because the professor was outstanding. Dr. Paul Boller was a young professor at the time, a Yale graduate. I loved the class, although not enough to change my major from comparative literature to history.

My admiration for Dr. Boller left me confused when one of the "yellow dog" Democrats in my sorority house informed me that Dr. Boller was a supporter of Adlai Stevenson. This was the first time I questioned my mother's assessment that all Democrats were low-class and stupid. I remained an admirer of President Eisenhower. It was a time for reflection and consolidation in America. Republicans would not have such a time again until Ronald Reagan appeared on the national scene. Unlike Reagan, Eisenhower had a clear and simple vision of what he did and did not want to accomplish. I think of him every time I begin a long driving trip on an Interstate highway. Also, under Eisenhower's administration, the Korean War finally ended in an armistice. I have often wondered what Eisenhower would have done with General MacArthur if Truman had not already fired him; I suspect Eisenhower would have done the same.

But college was certainly not all work and no play. I had learned in high school that making good grades could cover a multitude of sins. If you had the reputation of being a "brain" you could party, and no one paid much attention. In addition, I was always active on campus and at my church, the beautiful little St. Dunstan's Episcopal Chapel just off the main campus.

Alcohol was my joy and my passion. Accustomed to drinking wine and beer since I was sixteen, I gradually acquired a taste for Scotch whisky. I loved the feeling of freedom alcohol gave me. Whatever self-doubts I had melted with the first consumption of alcohol in any form. I was oblivious to the subtle effects of what is in reality a poison. There never seemed to be enough to satisfy me once I began to drink. The dangers were brought home to me on a couple of occasions when I could remember nothing of the end of the evening or how I got back to the sorority house.

I continued to get good grades and to be active on campus, although my drinking did not go unnoticed. When I was home, I always woke up my mother when I came in from a date. Often, I was too drunk to be cautious about talking to her and not drunk enough to realize it. After I married, she told me one day that she was afraid that when I was in college I would "become an alcoholic." Neither of us realized I already was one. I dated a lot, and in my junior and senior years mostly dated men who had already graduated. One who had spent two years in Korea would retire later as a Major General. A number of my dates had graduated from Princeton, and some from Yale. Many if not most of my friends joined the ROTC in college. Of course it helped pay the way through university, but most of the students simply assumed they would all have to go to war and preferred to serve as officers rather than as enlisted personnel. The Princeton graduates were all trained in artillery. Many were then posted to Fort Sill in Lawton, Oklahoma, for training. Fort Sill is an old and historic post where Geronimo spent his final days incarcerated by the Army. As interesting as the history of Fort Sill was, the young men from the East preferred to go to Dallas, a "great party town," on their weekends off rather than stay in Lawton or go to Oklahoma City in the "dry" state of Oklahoma.

The father of one of the men my sorority sisters and I dated was an executive with an oil company in Dallas. Although the young man never lived in Dallas, through friends of his parents he contacted one of my sorority sisters. Soon an entire cadre of Pi Beta Phi members was dating a group of Princeton men. I loved the wide-ranging conversations as well as the partying. I have wondered since then which—the parties or the conversations—were more important to me. The alcohol made me think I was a brilliant conversationalist.

None of this is to say I felt I had an inferior education or that there were no intellectuals on the SMU campus. I always considered it a gift that I went to SMU, which at the time had barely 3,000 students and an excellent faculty. I was able to have a great deal of personal attention in the classroom and to make myself known on the campus. The most broadly intellectual of my friends was a young man named Mortis Michaelson. Mortis had a job in the Comparative Literature Library, a small enclave in the huge Fondren Library. It was on the top floor, and I would often climb the stairs to visit with him. There were couches in the Comp Lit area, but usually we sat on the top of the metal fire escape stairs, smoked cigarettes, and talked.

Once he asked me to speak to a group of students who often met on Sundays for discussions. Most of them were graduate students. I accepted, and it became one of the more humiliating experiences of my life. First, I got lost trying to find the house in Plano where the meeting was held, so I was terribly late. Then I delivered what I considered my wonderful little paper, only to discover once the words were out of my mouth that the subject was banal in the extreme. The other students promptly ignored me and began discussing things that were far over my head. It is a wonder that the experience did not permanently sidetrack my efforts to address the public. The experience was properly humbling. Mortis was embarrassed for me, but he manfully kept up his end of our friendship until he left to study in Paris.

In the spring of 1954, I was tapped to become a member of Mortar Board, an honorary organization for senior women. During the summer I attended summer school as I had done the previous two summers. The following fall I finished my undergraduate work and enjoyed my first history course and a typing class. I signed up for a course in shorthand that I had to drop because I could not seem to make it to an eight o'clock morning class, and I was failing it anyway.

I also learned a valuable political lesson during my college years. If you want to run for office, prepare carefully. During my junior year I was house manager at my sorority. There was a good deal of responsibility involved, especially since the housemother retired every night around ten o'clock. I had to lock up the building on weekends and make sure all the women were inside. I also oversaw the renovation of the third floor of the building that turned what had been an attic into a study hall and chapter room where the sorority held initiations. The floor covering was a gift from my parents.

The sorority president at the time, Suzi Smith, took me aside one day and asked me if I wanted to serve as president. If I did, she said, I needed to start preparing. I declined. I was going to graduate early and did not want to stay on campus the extra semester. However, at the end of the year, for no apparent reason other than ego, I changed my mind. I ran and was defeated in a three-way contest. I filed all this away as good experience. As a consolation, they elected me song leader, and I became quite obnoxious in the job. From the time I was sixteen I sang in the church choir and even had private singing lessons during my high-school years: despite this, I had never really studied music. However, I had observed the way choral directors conducted, and I must have waved my arms around in a particularly exaggerated way. As a result, I was parodied by the pledge class in a skit they had prepared for the members. Perhaps it was a blessing for them and for me that I was not president.

In January, I returned to Oklahoma and, as if I had not had enough of school, promptly entered the graduate English Department at the University of Oklahoma (OU). I still thought I wanted to teach college English. The real reason I wanted to attend OU was because in the summer I had begun to date Boots Taliaferro, and he was seeing another woman. I went to OU to protect my turf. The effort yielded exactly three coffee dates with Boots, but I continued to see one of the Princeton men during the semester and seriously considered switching my attentions.

Boots continued to call me often; one Saturday night he called after a date. One of my roommates and I had spent the evening at our boarding house drinking martinis. Earlier we made a run to the river to buy a bottle of vermouth from a bootlegger. (The gin was easier to come by.) We mixed the drinks in fraternity mugs and ate smoked oysters as hors d'oeuvres. In the middle of my conversation with Boots I excused myself, went to the bathroom, and threw up the martinis. He was aware of what had gone on, so I blamed it on the oysters. He never ceased to tease me about this, even after my drinking had passed well beyond the amusing stage.

In addition to my social life, I took three courses: Renaissance English; an advanced course in Elizabethan English; and philosophy under Gustav Mueller, who at the time was the leading expert on Hegel.

That semester had a profound influence on me. During it, I was introduced to St. Anselm's ontological argument. Dr. Mueller was a meticulous teacher, and his exposition of the argument that God can be known only through analogy set me on what was the beginning of a spiritual journey.

From the time I was ten, I faithfully attended church with my mother. At SMU I was an active participant in the Episcopal church's campus organization. Part of my interest in the church stemmed from a quest to find some proof that God existed. I can only describe myself as more of a skeptic than a member of the faithful. After I studied with Dr. Mueller, I began to read in order to enhance what I knew then would always result in imperfect knowledge, but it was worth the effort. My spiritual journey has taken years and has had more than a few detours.

I also remember a disturbing conversation I had with Dr. Mueller. He was thoroughly convinced that the world was on the cusp of major sociological change and upheaval. He was desperately sad not to be young enough to live to see it. One of the silliest things that ever happened to me took place in graduate school. The Renaissance course I took had only six students—two women and four men. In the middle of the semester, each of us had to give a paper on something we had read, and I chose Wordsworth's long narrative poem *Peter Bell*, in which the eponymous character has a donkey that he rides on his journey. I was reading along and realized that the only other woman in the class was looking at me in horror while the four men and our professor were doubled up in laughter. In my own narrative, I had repeatedly described Peter as having "taken his ass" hither and yon. I suddenly realized what I was saying and laughed until the tears ran down my face. My presentation was obviously the high point of the semester.

That summer instead of going to school I spent the months working for my father. He had decided to set up a trust for Thurman and me. The corpus of the trust was to consist of the minerals he owned that were not presently producing oil or gas; that meant that he could make the gift without incurring any tax consequences. If the minerals produced later on, the income for the wells would be my brother's and mine. The trust would also hold the Norman real estate.

I learned the basics of the oil business. Most of the time I was typing mineral deeds on properties that would eventually be transferred to the trust. I worked on an ancient Remington typewriter that had no spell-check or correction capabilities and no memory but my own. One afternoon, a friend of my father who was in the oil business dropped by to chat. He asked my father, "Do you think your daughter would have time to come up and type a few deeds for me?" My father told him that I could if I wanted to, of course, but warned him that I typed at a high rate of speed and a low rate of accuracy. I spent one afternoon typing mineral deeds for the gentleman and earned my very first wages.

By the time summer came, Boots had stopped dating the other woman, and we were seeing each other regularly. He had plans to go to Europe with a friend for a month, and when he returned for his last year in law school we quickly decided to get married. Once again, I made a decision with security in mind rather than adventure. Carolyn Collier, my best friend from SMU, urged me to take a year off and go with her and other sorority sisters to New York to work. In some ways, I regret I missed the opportunity to be independent for a year instead of plunging directly into marriage. I doubt if anything except my self-confidence would have been affected. Since Boots needed to complete his last year of law school, he would have waited for me. Still, in all probability the quality of my life would have changed if I had made a different decision.

Chapter 8

MARRIED LIFE

WHEN HE PROPOSED, Boots gave me a lovely engagement ring his mother had bought several years earlier in hopes that he would get married. He proposed, and I accepted on a Saturday. My husband-to-be thought it appropriate to ask formally for my hand, so he asked if he could see my father on the following day. Never able to keep a secret, I had already told everyone anyway. My incomparable grandmother, who lived to be ninety-eight, made the first comment. I called her on Sunday morning before I went to church and said, "Grandmother, I'm going to get married." I could hear her draw in a quick breath. All she said was, "All those breakfasts." I had no inkling of what she was talking about, but in the years to come I would think of her while I was frying bacon and toasting bread.

After church, Boots came to the house for the meeting between the prospective groom and his father-in-law to be. Boots expected a private meeting, but as chance had it, my father was sitting in my mother's bedroom. Before Boots could begin, my grandmother and my uncle walked in on their usual Sunday afternoon visit with my invalid mother. To strain things further, my brother Thurman, his wife

Marilyn, and their eldest daughter had come to visit. It was almost as if the entire family had been telepathically alerted that something was up.

My mother waded into the discussion first and asked whether we planned to marry the following June, after Boots had graduated from law school. We said no, since he had bar exams then and Christmastime was too rushed. We planned to be married at Thanksgiving. Since it was already August, this plan put my mother in a state of shock. My father waited patiently for Boots to request my hand. Boots manfully began to explain that he felt he could afford to get married because he was a counselor in one of the freshman dormitories at the University of Oklahoma. This gave him board and room for himself and a spouse if he married. In addition, the university gave him a stipend of fifty dollars a month to buy food on the weekends when the university's cafeteria was closed and perhaps to see a movie or have a beer or two. He did not have to explain, but the income from my stock dividends would also help. In addition, we each owned our own automobiles. These arrangements may appear now to be a slender reed to support a marriage, but it seemed all right to us. My father listened soberly, giving the argument its due deference and agreed to the plan if it was what I truly wanted.

Planning for a large wedding at St. Paul's Episcopal Cathedral went on apace, and in my usual well-organized way, all was ready by the time the first party was scheduled for about three weeks before the wedding date of November 23. I went to the party, came home, and promptly threw up. This time the cause was not because I had had too much to drink. I had a swelling in my neck, and I thought I must have the flu because I ran a temperature. Instead, I had a dandy case of mononucleosis. My liver became involved, and my spleen swelled until the doctor was concerned that it might rupture. She put me in the hospital, mostly so I could be taken care of since my mother was not able to do so.

We sent out wedding cancellations. My mother-in-law cried for a day, my father retired to the office to get out of the fray, and I grew restless. My faithful bridegroom came to the hospital every day to visit, bringing me a pint of ice cream. It was the only time in my life I ate everything in sight and lost weight. Finally, when he came to see me a week before Thanksgiving, I suggested that he should get a marriage license so we could be married at home. He did, but not without difficulty. In those days, before you could get a license you had to take a test for syphilis, called a Wassermann test. The mono made me fail my test, so the hospital ran another more sensitive test to determine that I did not indeed have any loathsome disease.

However, this was not the end of our trials. On the wedding day, Boots's mother sewed me into my dress, because my spleen was still so swollen that I could not button it. We were married in the living room of my parents' home. There were fifteen people at the wedding, all family except for my friend Phyllis who played the piano, our best man Keith Hickox, and his wife Susan. In addition, there were my parents' friends, Bishop Chilton Powell and his wife, Betty. The Dean of the Cathedral performed the ceremony. The many clergy seemed like overkill, but the person who was really supposed to perform the ceremony was the priest from Saint Dunstan's in Dallas, Father Curt Junker, an old friend of the bishop. At the last minute Curt came down with pneumonia and could not attend.

The bishop attended in order to bless us after the conclusion of the ceremony. He went into my father's bathroom to put on his red robes, but the sliding door between the bedroom and bath stuck, and he could not get out. Finally, the groom, clad in a tuxedo, climbed through the bathroom window bearing a screwdriver and freed the then-vested clergy. All this was made worse when I was overcome with giggles during the vow "in sickness and in health." I was also so weak that I could not get up from the kneeler after the blessing. Boots got up, straddled the cathedral-length train of the dress, grabbed me under my arms, and hoisted me to my feet. I ate little of the dinner and retired immediately to bed, leaving the guests to have their own party. The morning after the ceremony, my father served the wedding couple breakfast in bed.

It was a comical beginning for a marriage that lasted for thirty years. As soon as I felt well enough, we took up residence at Bass House on the University of Oklahoma campus. The counselor's quarters consisted of sitting room, bedroom, and bath. We ate in the cafeteria. Since I had no meals to prepare or much housekeeping to attend to, I considered continuing graduate school, but I was still so weak that I decided to do nothing but recuperate.

I spent time as an unpaid secretary in the Law Review Office, but mostly I played bridge with other campus wives and read books. I also helped the freshman boys to prepare outlines for their English papers and ignored the beer they smuggled in. I refused to write the papers for them, a lucrative little business that some of the campus wives indulged in.

Boots graduated in June 1956; he passed the bar, and we bought our first house. Boots's family was in the cattle business, and his father had given him several head of cattle. The proceeds from selling that and from my stock investments made the down payment on a house that was nicer than the ones most of our friends owned. It was a charming, stacked-stone house with white trim, three bedrooms, a combination living room–dining room, a kitchen, and two full baths. All three of our children were born while we lived in what came to be known in our family as "the little house."

Boots got the best job of anyone in his graduating class. He joined the law firm of Monnet, Hayes, Bullis, Grubb, and Thompson and was paid $325.00 a month, which was then a princely sum.

Our daughter, Sarah, was born in August 1957, complete with two lower-incisor teeth. I was horrified when my mother suggested we contact the newspaper to take a picture and do a story on this remarkable infant with the precocious teeth. We had to have them pulled when she was about two weeks old so she could nurse, because they rubbed blisters on the bottom of her tongue.

These were the Eisenhower years. Everyone we knew was settling into the same sort of middle- and upper-class living our parents had achieved after the poverty of the Great Depression. Suburbia was taking shape. The automobile was king, and jobs were plentiful for working-class people. Two weeks of vacation time was usually spent driving somewhere. For us, vacation was often a drive to my family's Wisconsin summer home and back.

In the summer of 1958, my long-time friend Phyllis Cooper and her husband Dean Grewell persuaded us to leave our daughter Sarah with her Taliaferro grandparents and to visit them in Montana, where Dean was stationed in the Air Force. They would get a sitter for their son Rick, and we would camp and fish on the way to Lake Louise. We left Sarah with her grandparents and drove up the eastern slope of the Rocky Mountains from Denver. Then we went through Grand Teton and Yellowstone National Parks to Great Falls, Montana. We spent the night with the Grewells, and the next day we threw everything into their white Dodge station wagon, including Boots's 25-horsepower Johnson motor with its remote gas tank. The two men cursed the motor every time they needed to open the back end of the station wagon to get anything or to remove the camping gear to pitch camp.

"Why did we bring that damned motor?" they groused. "We probably won't have time to use it to fish anyway."

The first night together, we camped somewhere in Canada. This was after the border guards confiscated Boots' pistol, which he insisted on bringing along, unaware that no one could take firearms into Canada. By this time I had caught a head cold, and the men decided to treat me with the "old Indian cure"—a pint of whiskey. They drove to town and purchased a pint of Canadian whiskey, which is made from rye. Although I had drunk more than my share of booze over time, I had drunk rye only once, and it had made me deathly ill. This was the second time, and it had the same result. The following morning, they carted me off to Calgary Hospital to a doctor who gave me a shot of penicillin for the cold and nothing for the hangover.

We drove up through Glacier National Park to Lake Louise. We were too poor to do anything but enjoy the spectacular view, which we did, leaving the station wagon unattended. It was the only time during that day I was out of the car. While we were gone, someone put something into the gas tank of the car as a prank. We did not know this until the car stopped running when we were approximately a quarter of the way down the western slope of the Continental Divide in Alberta. This is the less-traveled part of the mountains, and the only place we could stop was an overlook with a small gas station. There was no help there, so we coasted down the mountain into a small town. It was not an encouraging sign to see that the Royal Canadian Mounted Police station was boarded up.

The men found a park in which to pitch camp, and Phyllis took me to the only hotel in town. The men located a one-man garage. That one man's solution to our problem was to pick up a sledgehammer and a crowbar from the tool bin; our husbands thanked him politely and said they thought they might be able to fix the problem themselves. Meanwhile, Phyllis installed me into the hotel. It was an old house with rooms to rent, and we laughed over the decor. The owner obviously loved roses and, given the short northern growing season, decided to bring her passion indoors using ersatz roses. They were everywhere. The floor was covered with an old linoleum rug that had a border of red roses and an arrangement of roses in the center. The chintz draperies were printed with red roses. The wallpaper had more roses. None of the patterns matched or came close to coordination. I felt like a beetle inside a rose bush. But the place was warm, had sunny windows, and was immaculately clean. Perhaps heaven is being a beetle inside a rose bush.

Dean Grewell was nothing if not resourceful. The men discovered that the car's fuel pump was working, but the gasoline was not reaching it. Surmising there was a clog in the line, Dean took the much-maligned remote gas can from the Johnson motor, put it on the floor of the front right seat, and ran the fuel line through the car's fire wall. He then attached it to the fuel pump and *voila*—the car ran just fine. However, the station wagon used so much gasoline we had to stop to refuel every thirty miles. For the rest of the trip, I was the designated navigator and plotted our next pit stop. It always took a lot of time to get gas. We would begin by signaling the attendant to come to the front seat. They would nod, disbelieving, and start for the rear of the car. "No, no," we would explain. "You have to fill the tank on the floor of the front seat." Then we would have to tell the entire story.

There were rules, too. All of us smoked at the time. "No smoking in the seats" was rule number one. So each time we wanted a cigarette, the smoker had to climb over the gear in the back of the station wagon and the outboard motor, open the back window, and smoke while hanging out of the rear of the car.

We finally finished our trip. The one night we could afford to stay indoors we spent at Waterton Lakes in Canadian Glacier Park, one of the places on earth I still dream about. At that time, the town was small and delightfully English and had lots of shops. The lodge was wonderful in an early twentieth-century rustic way. The lake view was almost as nice as Lake Louise's and much more intimate.

We nearly had two disasters there. First, the men went upstream to fish while Phyllis and I showered and shopped. They let the sun go down before they headed back and were truly afraid they would not make it out of the river's steep canyon without daylight. They did make it back with one fish. For some reason I remember cleaning it at the lakeshore, but I don't remember what we did with it. Then, as we were packing the car, Dean threw away some papers in the roaring fire in the lobby of the inn. Although Boots' pistol was waiting for us to pick up on our way back into the United States, we still had ammunition in the car. Somehow a bullet had gotten into the wastepaper, and it exploded in the fire. Dean and I looked at each other, horrified. Luckily it did not send the projectile into the room to hit another hapless guest or us. We left the hotel in a hurry.

We finally returned safely to Great Falls and unloaded the station wagon. Dean, sitting in the middle of the living room, looked at the pile of things that we had hauled and said, "What idiot thought they could get all of that stuff and four people in one car?" But we had, and the hated Johnson outboard proved to be essential.

This was the first but not the last of those driving vacations when Boots and I tossed the kids in the car and dragged them off to see the world—or at least, the United States. But this trip was the most memorable.

A few months before I was editing this book Phyllis Cooper Grewell, my oldest friend and companion on that trip, died just after my ninety-first birthday and just before hers. Later in the summer I was surprised by a visit at the lake house from her oldest child, Rick. We had a wonderful visit full of memories. I asked him, "Did your folks ever tell you about our trip to Canada?" "Oh, yes. Often," was his response.

•••

The final five years of the 1950s were placid. I do not believe I have ever seen a time of such style and beauty. Clothing was exquisitely designed and beautifully made. Fashion was important; trends were set in Paris and New York and then watched and followed everywhere in small and large cities. The graphic and plastic arts were less beautiful than the clothes of the day, but they reflected the influence of new thinking. Furniture design showed an acceptance of the Bauhaus school, and non-objective art was making its appearance. Op Art, with its dizzying patterns, also had a short run of popularity.

More importantly, for the first time perhaps ever in the United States, average citizens had the money to begin to realize their dreams. Thanks to the G.I. bill and dozens of other pieces of legislation, affordable housing and funding for small businesses were available to those who wanted to take advantage of the growing economy and the government's services.

My experience growing up with working-class children and my brief introduction to racism brought an awakening. After watching McCarthy and his callow antics, I paid more attention to what was going on in Washington, DC. I realized I did not share many of the views of my more conservative parents. Boots was a Democrat, and I concluded, so was I. On the other hand, the Taliaferros were Methodists, and Boots was an observant one. I continued to attend the Episcopal Church nearly every Sunday, especially after I became pregnant with our first child, Sarah. Eventually, after many conversations with The Rev. Russell Rauscher, rector of All Soul's Church, Boots was confirmed in the Episcopal church. Once, when my mother was chiding him about his political ideas and what she considered his undue influence over my thinking, she admonished him, "And you've made her a *Democrat*." "Well, Crete, as for influence, I am not longer a Methodist. I am an Episcopalian," was his response. She retorted, "I guess that shows your primary loyalty lies with politics and not your faith."

Boots also made a baseball fan of me. One of my outstanding memories is of watching Don Larson pitch the only perfect game in a World Series in 1956. The Dodgers' Dale Mitchell, from Oklahoma, was the last batter up against the Yankees, and I secretly wanted him to hit a home run. He did not, and I was overwhelmed with the idea that I had the privilege of sitting in my living room and watching a history-making event, still never equaled—the only perfect game in World Series history.

By the end of the 1950s, television had become an integral part of life. Much of what was shown was unremarkable, but there was some really good content. Live television drama was as close to going to the theater as many of us could get. And it was a time when the news broadcasts were still focused on public affairs rather than on entertainment. Boots and I closely watched the approaching election season leading up to the 1960 campaign. He was still a fan of Adlai Stevenson. I had been impressed by John Kennedy's close try for the Vice-Presidential slot when Stevenson had thrown open the 1956 convention instead of naming his running mate. I did not want to see Stevenson nominated for a third time, because I felt he had proved to be unelectable. My favorite was Senator Lyndon B. Johnson; I admired his ability to get things done. He was a masterful politician and knew Congress as well as anyone ever had. My only concern was whether a southerner could be elected. But then, he was a Texan, and as *tout le monde* knows, Texans are different.

We watched, reserving judgment. The fifties slid seamlessly into 1960. It was an enormous threshold, and few people recognized it. I believe it is only now as I write this book that I can appreciate the gulf we crossed. The bridge over it seemed so sturdy and timeless.

Chapter 9

PASSING THE TORCH

IN 1956, WHEN then-Governor of Illinois Adlai E. Stevenson ran for a second time against Dwight Eisenhower for the presidency of the United States, I learned what I then believed was my first and last political lesson. As I look back, it was neither the first nor the last lesson in what I have finally accepted as an education that began long before I was aware of political parties or the electoral process. I thought it all began and ended as I stood in the kitchen of our home and heard the door open when my husband Boots came home from work. I said, "I will never, *ever*, do anything in a political campaign again." I made this assertion with anger, passion, and more than a few tears. I meant every word.

Before we married the previous year, I extracted a solemn promise from my fiancé that he would never engage in what I considered the dirty game of politics. He had been a big man on campus, and even his closest friends often referred to him playfully as "the senator." He assured me he intended to practice law the rest of his life in the firm that had hired him when he graduated from law school. These promises were made and extracted with the best of intentions and with the complete ignorance of young people who assume they are adults and wise in all things. We inevitably learned, through the growing reality of each successive year, just how wrong such youthful assumptions could be.

In 1956 we went to downtown Oklahoma City to a reception for Governor Stevenson. I was impressed with his intelligence, earnestness, humor—and his exhaustion. His face was flushed and alert, and his gray suit was wrinkled. "Campaigning must be a wearing business," I thought. Caught up in the fever of a presidential election, my husband and William J. Holloway, Jr., volunteered to help.

We lived not just in conservative Oklahoma City but also in the silk-stocking area of town, a deeply Republican district, although everyone in those days registered as a Democrat in order to have some say in local and state government. The suburb, which was also an incorporated town, was well-educated and self-satisfied. This was the area the men had volunteered to canvass for Stevenson. We gathered at the elder Holloway's home to discuss plans. The number of Stevenson supporters would have filled two bridge tables.

I thought as a proper wife that I should help, and I meekly took on the task my husband had volunteered to do: phoning our neighbors to urge them to vote for Stevenson. The day I did that standing in the kitchen, three people hung up on me. The last woman I had talked to harangued me until I cried. She lectured me about the evils of Governor Stevenson and his presumptuousness in running against the sainted President Eisenhower.

Those tears did not last long, and my resolve to avoid politics survived only until John Fitzgerald Kennedy rose to make his acceptance speech at the 1960 Democratic convention in Los Angeles. With the election of John Kennedy in 1960, America slipped easily over a cultural divide without a ripple. However, there had been signs even in the 1950s of a restless, changing country: the sit-ins and the bus boycott; the rise of Joseph McCarthy; and the quiet integration of the Theology School at SMU. The smooth patina of the fifties was dumped onto a food blender; it emerged not pureed but chopped into pieces.

Change came slowly and subtly. In the summer of 1960, just after our second child, Henry, was born, Boots and I went to San Francisco for a couple of weeks. We spent much of our time in the North End. We hung out in the "beat" cafes and coffee houses and listened to the Smothers Brothers at the Hungry I. The music was fresh—some folk, some country, some reminiscent of the rhythm and blues I heard at the bars close to the SMU campus I used to frequent. One opener, I believe for The Kingston Trio, was the wonderful country singer Charlie Pride. Hearing that glorious voice, no one noticed that he was Black.

About this time, Boots' fraternity asked three or four couples to chaperone one of their dances. At our age, "chaperone" was a dubious description. It had more to do with our being over the age of twenty-one to watch all the underage drinkers. The party was held on a Santa Fe Railway train. The idea of a "train party" originated with one of our friends whose father was on the board of the Santa Fe Railway. He rented a string of rail cars for the occasion, including a boxcar to house a band for dancing, a bar car for the drinks, and a chair car for sitting. These train cars were hauled behind a long freight train that left Oklahoma City early in the evening. When we reached Arkansas City, Kansas, our cars were decoupled and switched onto a siding to be picked up by a southbound train sometime after midnight.

The women in our chaperone group arrived dressed in their best black cocktail dresses, stockings, and black strap sandals. College students in those days were not dressed in blue jeans. They dressed like us, but their actions were completely different. The chaperones were still dancing the Lindy and the two-step. The students were doing something entirely different; they never touched each other; we were used to dancing cheek to cheek. One of the dances was the Watusi, and I remember looking at the dancers and thinking that they were from some strange and foreign culture. Their actions seemed inexplicable. Was this really fun?

***

It would not be long before students shed the existing dress codes and shed their inhibitions as well. Underneath what might have looked familiar to us early in the 1960s was a profound change, The pill to prevent conception had become readily available; we were the last generation before the sexual revolution. Later on, most of us used the pill for birth control, but by the time it appeared, we had already gone through our primary dating and pairing stages and had carried on courtship with a lot of heavy foreplay that rarely ended in sexual intercourse.

The threat of AIDS and sexually transmitted diseases now seems to have changed the mores, but for the young people of the 1960s and the 1970s, all you needed, as my daughter put it, was to be "somewhere comfortable." If the sexual revolution did not have much of an impact on my generation, a much more obvious political change did: Democrats once more had the White House. We were happy about this, but our conversion to being devotees of John F. Kennedy was a reluctant process.

In March of 1960, Kennedy's victory in the West Virginia primary impressed Boots and me. To many voters and the press, it proved that Kennedy could win as a Roman Catholic in a primarily rural state. The principal architect of that victory was Matt Reese. Matt and his wife Martha would become our personal friends, and he was my principal mentor.

As impressive as his West Virginia victory was, we still had personal reservations about Kennedy. He was young, untried, relatively unknown, the son of the notorious old Joe Kennedy, and a Roman Catholic. Later, after the time of the civil-rights movement, the doubts about his religion would seem silly to us, but in the days before Pope John XXIII took charge, the Catholic Church was deeply conservative. We had no idea how Kennedy felt about the church's influence on public policy. We were skeptical. As the primary campaign progressed, Boots still hoped that Adlai Stevenson would again be the nominee, and I continued to root for Senator Lyndon B. Johnson.

The real turning point for us was Kennedy's acceptance speech at the convention. Sitting in our living room before the boxy television set, we were spellbound. The combination of his striking presence, assisted by Ted Sorenson's speechwriting, was electric. Later, Kennedy's straightforward speech to some Baptist ministers in Houston reconfirmed our support. For me, Kennedy's choice of Lyndon Johnson as his vice president was an act of political courage and grace. To choose as a running mate a former opponent as formidable as Johnson took great self-confidence.

By the time the fall campaign came around, I could carve out enough time from caring for babies to help with some fundraising. Boots did what he could to help the party, and we both made it a point to go to the rally for Kennedy at the municipal auditorium. Kennedy was there with two of his sisters, and my impression of all of them was as vivid as the colors the ladies wore. All of us wore our best two-piece wool suits. Mine was black; theirs were orange and grass green. I filed the wearing of rich colors away as a piece of campaign wisdom for political wives—wear something simple and bright so people can see you.

We felt that Kennedy was one of us. The impression he gave of youth and vitality came from a personality that radiated to a crowd. After the speech we ran down the street, chasing the convertible he rode in to get a closer look. I saw him off-stage only twice: the day he appeared in Oklahoma City and the day he died, and both times he was in the back seat of an open car.

Election night was an ordeal. Several couples among us young Democrats rented a suite at the old Skirvin Tower Hotel in downtown Oklahoma City. As the hours went on, the tension became unbearable. The prospect of Richard Nixon as president was unthinkable. For us, some of his campaign consultants, such as Murray Chotiner, were in the same class as Joseph McCarthy; they were untrustworthy xenophobes. Years later Murray and Nancy Chotiner would be our neighbors. One Christmas, Murray and I sat around our kitchen table lustily singing Christmas carols. I was astounded that Murray, a devout Jew, knew the words and the tunes of every carol we sang.

About two o'clock in the morning after election day, I tried to sleep but couldn't breathe. Boots took me to the emergency room at Saint Anthony's Hospital a few blocks away. The harassed ER doctor could find nothing wrong with me. My own diagnosis is that I was probably close to alcohol poisoning. (I usually drank a steady diet of Scotch whisky from early evening until after midnight.) We returned to our hotel, and I passed out on the bed, fully clothed. Early in the morning, the men woke those of us who had not gone home to tell us Kennedy had finally won. We watched on television the acceptance speech he delivered from Hyannis Port. We observed with the same interest his choice of cabinet members and, finally, his marvelous speech at the inaugural ceremony. As much as we wanted to go to Washington for it, we couldn't afford the cost or the time away from the children.

I am always wryly amused when I hear Republicans quote either FDR or John Kennedy. One day I may live long enough to hear one of them quote Bill Clinton or Barack Obama. My strongest memories of the Kennedy era are of the hate shown him by Republicans. Few presidents have been as hated and vilified by the opposition as John Kennedy. In all honesty, his presidency did not start well; the Bay of Pigs incident made a poor beginning. The best that can be said about it was that it showed Kennedy's grace under pressure. Coming from such a young chief executive, this was welcome reassurance.

We would see the same sort of calm assurance during the Cuban missile crisis. Kennedy addressed the nation about the prospect of nuclear weapons being stored within close range of our cities. Tapes of the speech are available, and they show a president who was decisive and confident. He began by citing his legal authority to impose what he called a "quarantine" on Russian shipping. He went on to emphasize the regional nature of the crisis and related it to the global alliances the US had made with NATO, the United Nations, and the Organization of American States. One of the points he made was that to do nothing was not a winning strategy and that unprovoked aggression was never acceptable.

For those of us who remembered World War II and the fear that we would be bombed, the prospect of having bombs at our back door was terrifying. I had two small children, and I revisited all my feelings about August 1945. I found myself wondering where we would hide. My sister-in-law Marilyn and I bought canned goods in bulk along with bottled water. We discussed building a bomb shelter in the back yard. Many people did just that. I felt helpless in a way I had not felt since the bombs fell on Pearl Harbor, on Hiroshima and Nagasaki, and three years later when the Russians detonated a nuclear device. These were the emotional peaks of Kennedy's short presidency, but my real impression was based less on his administrative accomplishments and more on his style and grace. His contribution was one of focus, vision, and inspiration. The seniority system in Congress was in full force. It would take Lyndon Johnson, who knew the ins and outs of Congressional rules, personalities, commitments, and quirks to bring about real legislative change. It was almost as though the times demanded that Kennedy serve as the strategist and Johnson as the tactician—two halves of a whole to move the country forward. It was a vision greatly helped and articulated by Robert F. Kennedy. John Kennedy, along with his wife Jacqueline, gave many in our generation a sense of purpose. His death deepened the personal resolve of many of us to serve the state. For Boots and me, it changed our lives.

Chapter 10

DALLAS

THE DEATHS OF my parents are indelibly associated with President Kennedy's assassination in November 1963. My father died ten months before in January 1963, and my mother died twenty months afterwards in the summer of 1965. My father suffered a stroke in December, and I accompanied him to the hospital. My brother was in Taiwan on business, so I spent as much time at the hospital as I could. The second week in January, he was slated to be released on a Wednesday. In the early hours of that day, I received a call from the hospital. He had died of a massive stroke at about three o'clock in the morning.

After my father's death, I discovered that I was pregnant with our youngest child, William. That spring and fall I was busy redoing my parents' house so we could move into it with our three children and take care of my mother. I had promised my father that I would see to her care. Will was born in August, we moved in September, and on November 21 Boots and I went to Dallas for the weekend to celebrate our wedding anniversary,

The year before, on the same weekend, we had gone to Dallas with our friends Jim and Charlotte Little. Charlotte and I had a friend, Noreen Haynes, who had recently moved from Oklahoma City to Dallas. As a Dallas Southern Methodist University alumna, I thought it would be nice to invite friends from school to lunch at the Zodiac Room at the Neiman Marcus department store and introduce our friend. I invited about eight of my sorority sisters; two of the women were Phi Beta Kappa members.

At the lunch, I discovered that our friend had already met several of the women. On its surface, Dallas was a friendly town where Southern hospitality went hand in hand with Texas openness. The conversation at lunch was bizarre. One of my Phi Beta Kappa friends inveighed against Earl Warren and said she had an "Impeach Earl Warren" sticker on her car. Someone else at the table said "Assassinate Earl Warren" was a better fate for the Chief Justice than impeachment. By the time the luncheon was over I was in shock. Later when we discussed that luncheon among ourselves, Noreen, a native Californian, was aghast. Her father, a prominent Republican, was a long-time supporter of Warren when he was Governor of California and when he later served in the Senate.

These were the years when the John Birch Society heavily influenced Texas politics. Boots and one of his law partners, John Wagner (a Republican), had attended a Birch Society meeting in Oklahoma City. As Boots later told the story, he and John thought they were both very smart in voicing their opposition to the jingoism that the Birchers endorsed. As they were leaving the meeting, they noticed a small group of people who were not convinced by the Birchers' brilliant rhetoric. John remarked that it seemed as though the only thing their argument had accomplished was to identify the hardcore ultra-right participants. John speculated that the only thing their attend the meeting had accomplished was to winnow out the true believers. However, they also came away convinced that the John Birch movement had no future in Oklahoma City because although E.K. Gaylord, the arch-conservative publisher of the *Daily Oklahoman*, might have been an eccentric, he did not like people he considered nuts. Gaylord ran the town to his own liking, and in this case he was an ameliorating factor.

The atmosphere in Dallas was different from what it was in Oklahoma City. Although it was also deeply conservative, Dallas tolerated the sort of open hostility that resulted in Lady Bird Johnson's being spat upon at a downtown hotel. This hostility had not diminished between 1962 and 1963, when we once more went to Dallas with the Littles. We stayed at the Adolphus Hotel and spent Thursday evening at a supper club.

On Friday morning Boots and I got up, dressed, and watched the President and Mrs. Kennedy on television during their appearances in Fort Worth. We prepared to go to Neiman Marcus to shop. The *Dallas Morning News* was at the door, and we looked at it before we left the room. The President's schedule and the route of his motorcade were on the front page. The newspaper went into great detail about the coming events. We calculated when the parade might pass Neiman's and went on to meet the Littles for breakfast.

The store opened about ten, I bought a purse, and we all went to the women's shoe department. Charlotte and I did not buy any shoes, but the windows there looked out onto Commerce Street. It was a great vantage point from which to watch the parade. People crowded the windows in the buildings on the other side of the street. For some reason I found myself scanning the rooftops on those buildings. I suppose it was not really a premonition but a rather normal act for someone who was about to watch a presidential parade.

We waved and cheered; we had a wonderful view. I especially remember the roses; Mrs. Kennedy had brilliant

American Beauty roses that complemented her strawberry pink suit trimmed in navy blue. Mrs. Johnson's roses were yellow, and she wore beige clothing. After the parade passed, we went on with our shopping, and I found a beautiful black *peau de soie* dress. It had two pieces and was made in the simple style that Jacqueline Kennedy popularized. I was having it fitted when Boots found me and said, "Something has happened."

The president had been shot, and the report was picked up from a television on the floor of the men's department. Every emergency vehicle in the city must have converged on downtown with its sirens on, and the din was incredible. I hurriedly made my purchase of the dress as the salesgirl moaned in a corner of the dressing room "Why Dallas?" "Where else?" I snapped at her, remembering the luncheon conversation of a year before. I went to join Charlotte and the men. We watched the broadcast until the President's death was announced. The store's loudspeaker repeated the news, summoned all the employees to the first floor, and said the store was closing. We were almost the last customers to leave, and a man we assumed to be Stanley Marcus was solemnly addressing all of the employees as everyone filed out of the building.

With no clear idea of what to do next, the four of us went out to St. Michael and All Angels Episcopal Church. It was deserted but open. The altar was already draped in the black veil used on Good Friday. Later we went to the Plaza, ate lunch, and walked around aimlessly. The city, so cacophonous earlier, was as quiet as on a Sunday. I remember looking up into the cloudless blue sky and seeing a lone white airplane. By then I had lost all concept of time and wondered whether it was Air Force One carrying the new President Johnson, President Kennedy's body, and the two wives. Walking back to the hotel that afternoon, Boots and I made a promise to each other that we would not abandon the vision President Kennedy had given us. That promise would take us on a long journey.

We kept abreast of the news about the chase for and the capture of Lee Harvey Oswald at the movie theater as well as all the false reports made in between. In the evening we went to dinner somewhere and tried to salvage the weekend without much success. I kept remembering the luncheon I had attended in Dallas a year earlier and the hatred I had witnessed. Today's tragedy began to have both a surreal aspect and a feeling of inevitability like a Greek tragedy.

The following morning, I turned on the television to watch the news. Boots went into the bathroom to shower and shave. He was shaving when the footage showed deputies transferring Oswald from the Dallas County Jail to a Federal facility. "Someone's going to shoot that guy," I remarked in a rather matter-of-fact way. Then there was the gunshot. "There it is," I said. Boots rushed out of the bathroom, and we watched as the wounded Oswald was carried away. This was the last chapter in a tragic weekend. Years later, during the O.J. Simpson murder trial, I wrote an article about the assassination of Kennedy for the *Oklahoma Gazette*. My hope was that O.J.'s very public murder trial would restore a measure of confidence to the legal system.

The premise of my article was that two acts—the shooting of Oswald and Ford's late pardon of Richard Nixon—did enormous damage to the public's perception of a working legal system and a working political system in the United States. Jack Ruby's shooting of Oswald precluded a fair and open trial for the assassin and helped spawn all the later conspiracy theories.

President Ford's pardon of Richard Nixon, despite his best motives, precluded the open investigation of the charges against Nixon and covered up what was probably the most egregious misuse of power ever perpetrated by a United States president. Some would later argue the Iran-Contra affair was even worse, but what happened on January 6, 2021 was simply beyond comprehension at the time.

Chapter 11

MY DAYS IN COURT

DURING THE SIXTIES I had two experiences of my own with the legal system. The first was serving as a juror on a federal case. Ted Davis, one of Boots's law-school buddies, was then Clerk of the Federal Court in Oklahoma City. I believe he made sure I was in the jury pool after I once told him I had an interest in serving. By pure chance I ended up on the jury of a conspiracy trial. A high-school friend of mine, Carolyn Compton, was also chosen to serve. I was surprised that the judge left me on the panel since I was the wife of an attorney. I was not really acquainted with any of the attorneys in the case, so I was not challenged.

Another friend was not so lucky. Her husband was also an attorney. Because they had no children, the couple had an active social life. One of their buddies was an attorney for the defendant. On voir dire (the preliminary questioning of jurors to assess their ability to serve), the judge asked her whether she knew any of the attorneys, and she said yes. "Which one?" he asked. She indicated the gentleman.

"How do you know him?" asked Judge Wallace, a very strait-laced Baptist.

"Socially," she said.
"What do you mean?"
"We belong to the same club."
"What club?"

Instead of the Rotary Club or one of the many social dance clubs, or a country club, she finally named one of the quasi-legal drinking clubs around town. In the early 1960s you could not sell liquor in Oklahoma. The judge dismissed her.

The jury experience was one of the most uplifting of my life. There were seven or eight defendants, including the Mayor and the Police Chief of Lawton, Oklahoma. The suit was brought in Federal Court not because the charge was bootlegging but because the liquor was sold without a federal stamp. Beer of no more than 3.2 percent alcohol content was for sale in "tap rooms" or so-called "supper clubs" and in bars. More importantly, no wine or hard liquor could be sold legally in the state. Thus, there was a thriving business for bootleggers. Whiskey was brought into the state and sold, which was a convenience for most of us, like the dairy delivering milk. You just called up and ordered what you wanted, and it was delivered to your door. You could even call in an order if you ran out of booze at a party, and the person driving around to bring the stuff was a sober driver, often better dressed than many party guests.

Most of the state authorities looked the other way. However, the US Bureau of Alcohol, Tobacco, and Firearms (ATF) would intervene if it thought it could make a case. Lawton, Oklahoma, was close enough to the Texas border to be a convenient hub for bootlegging whiskey. Fort Sill was there, and this federal institution was the site of the major business of the town. Then the ATF stepped in. The main witness for the prosecution was a crusty old ATF man right out of central casting. He was about fifty, was a little overweight and wore a rumpled gray suit. He had a dead-on delivery as he responded to the questions he was asked. I was fascinated by his tale of the investigation and its discoveries. In those days, it was rumored that the "revenooers" (ATF) and the bootleggers did not go armed with guns or at least did not use them. There was an unspoken agreement that bootleggers would be safe from harm as long as they did not show a weapon. Otherwise, they were summarily shot by the law, or so the story went.

There must have been eight or ten lawyers for the defense. The slight, courtly Republican gentleman who was the Federal District Attorney presented the State's case. The trial went on for a week. We were not sequestered, but we were charged by the judge not to read the newspapers. I was careful to follow his instructions, but I asked Boots to save all the papers so I could read them after the trial. In the jury room we elected a foreman and quickly found all but three of the defendants guilty as charged on all counts. The remaining three included the driver of the truck carrying the booze, the mayor, and the police chief.

We took the case of the young driver first. He had done the job for money, and there was no indication that he was in on the planning. One of the jurors was a wheat farmer from Yukon, west of Oklahoma City. He did not think it was fair to convict the driver simply for taking a job. I remember the farmer, neatly dressed in khaki pants and shirt, gazing pensively out of the window while others argued against his position. He had a strong profile and skin like saddle leather. We were twelve people who took the job seriously, and the wheat farmer in my view was the outstanding member of the jury. The argument on the other side was that the driver had to know what he was transporting; thus he was at least an accomplice. We finally reached a guilty verdict for the driver, but I don't think we found him guilty of all charges.

Then the tough deliberations over the sheriff and the mayor, the two remaining defendants, began. Judge Wallace in his instructions to the jury was meticulous in describing what he considered to be "beyond reasonable doubt." We took his charge seriously. We argued for hours, went back into the courtroom to have testimony read to us, and adjourned that day without a verdict. The next day we argued some more. Carolyn and I were especially passionate about the State's case. The farmer joined us. Surely, we thought, both men were guilty, but in these deliberations opinions did not necessarily count. We considered the state's evidence to be paper thin, and we did not believe they had made their case. Eventually, we found the men innocent on all counts. This was the way the system was supposed to work. If the prosecution can't make a case fair and square, the defendant goes free. In this way, everyone's freedom is protected.

The second time I had an encounter with the justice system, I was, in a way, the defendant. My father died in January 1963, and my mother died in August 1965, not quite three years later. The Internal Revenue Service had then, and still has, a three-year window to question whether or not financial arrangements concerning an estate made prior to someone's death were made "in contemplation of death." The IRS and the State of Oklahoma insisted that we owed a great deal more in inheritance tax on my father's original estate than we maintained we owed. Although much of the estate came to my brother Thurman and me in trust, my father had a lot in his own name, which my mother, my brother Thurman, and I inherited directly. After Mother died, we paid what the IRS said we owed. Then we sued the federal government and the state of Oklahoma to recover a portion of the tax; we maintained that the plans for her estate were made not in "contemplation of death," but in "contemplation of life." The plans were made so she could be taken care of as long as she lived, whether it was for one, three, or ten years.

The federal case was a bench trial before Judge Fred Daugherty. His handling of the case was quiet and, I thought, masterful. One of the witnesses for our side was our father's accountant, who helped us all with our estate planning after our father died. He came up with a fair formula for us to divide the property and to allow Boots and me to move into my mother's house to see to her care. Thurman and my Uncle Charles testified as trustees of the Myers Trust. Boots and my mother's physician also testified. I was the last witness, and I felt as though I was the defendant in the witness box. Although I had given a deposition previously, I was unprepared for the emotional trauma of testifying on the stand. It made me relive all the grief brought on by my mother's years of illness and her terrible death. What I remember most about my testimony was my angrily denying that she was fat, and my describing how light she was when we had to restrain her during the final two weeks of her life. The hemorrhaging in her brain made her psychotic at the end, and she imagined she could get up and walk after ten years of invalidism. After I was dismissed, I went into the hall alone and sobbed by the window with its ornate iron bars.

The judge found in our favor. Before we left the courthouse, the attorney for the US Justice Department, who was from Washington, approached me in the lobby of the Federal Courthouse. "I apologize to you," he said and then added, "I hate these cases." I could understand, but I also knew it was a job that had to be done. The government is charged with keeping all of us honest. The state's portion of our suit went all the way to the Oklahoma Supreme Court.

As I mentioned earlier, in the conspiracy case we jurors had not been allowed to read the newspapers. When

I read the papers Boots had saved for me that had coverage of the conspiracy case, I wondered what trial the reporters had attended. There was absolutely no similarity between my impressions of what happened and what was reported. In our tax case, the interest of the press extended beyond Oklahoma. It was unusual for anyone to win a contemplation-of-death suit, so our victory in federal court made the front page of *The Wall Street Journal*. Even in such an august newspaper, there were so many inaccuracies I could scarcely recognize the case. It taught me a lot about journalism, journalists, and reporting. A report, even from an experienced reporter, consists only of snapshots. Often the complete picture is entirely different.

Chapter 12

LEARNING THE TRADE

MY POLITICAL LIFE began in earnest during the almost three years we lived with my mother. I had three young children, a husband who liked things "just so," and, because of the size of the house and Mother's illness, a staff of servants. Although my relationship with Mother was good and my marriage was reasonably happy despite all the family stress, I found I had to get out of the house. Singing in the church choir and doing my Junior League work were only marginally satisfying.

In the summer of 1964, as Fred Harris' primary campaign for the Senate was underway, Harris' Oklahoma County campaign manager Eugene Matthews asked me to work full-time in the Harris campaign. Fred was running to fill the unexpired term left when Senator Kerr died. As Eugene explained, he needed me because he had two women, one in the headquarters and one working with volunteers, who did not get along with each other. Would I come in as the peacemaker and also help in the organization? I said yes, not so much because I wanted the job but because I needed time away from the house. Political campaigns were just the ticket. They were short, and most of the long hours of work took place between the primary and the general elections. Campaigns had a beginning and a definite end, which I liked. Since they ended in November, I would have plenty of time to plan for Christmas. They were also stimulating, and I believed I would be doing a civic service, something I still believe.

Although I liked the people drawn to campaigns and I still do, I was less enthralled with the candidates themselves. Some I liked for themselves or for their talents; others I did not care for at all but supported as long as I thought they were competent, honest, and well-meaning. I have great sympathy and respect for the families and spouses who have to go through the ordeal of campaigns and elections. Mother did not share my enthusiasm for politics and took some pleasure in having me help her mark her absentee ballot in the general election for Fred Harris' opponent, the former football coach at the University of Oklahoma, Bud Wilkinson. This first Harris campaign was where I began my in-depth political training.

The real bonus was meeting John Robert Kennedy ("Bob" to his friends). He was no relation to the president, but he was a huge admirer of the nationally known John and Robert Kennedy. Bearing their names and being their age seemed to give him an added reason to pursue political involvement. Bob was the brains of Fred Harris's county campaign. A former (and future) Republican, he had worked in the Eisenhower campaigns in Montana, where he lived at the time, and worked as a geologist after graduating from Princeton and receiving an MBA from Harvard.

For the first time as Democrats we had real block captains and real canvassers. There were no readily available materials for a campaign in those days before computers, but we did have photocopiers. We took the Criss-Cross Directory for Oklahoma City. and Bob copied every page at least once, and twice for the pages containing addresses that bordered precinct lines. This was all done at night in the offices of the Eason Oil Company where he worked. All of us thought his boss, Winston Eason, probably knew he was making a substantial—and substantially illegal—contribution to a campaign. Perhaps he thought of it as a personal rather than corporate contribution. We were grateful and did not question things too closely.

My job was to staff the headquarters with volunteers, train them to underline the proper addresses, and assemble walk sheets for the canvassers. We were like the bumblebees; we didn't know we couldn't fly, so we did. A recent Harvard graduate was in charge of assigning canvassers, making sure they had yard signs, and organizing them to hit the streets. Fred was already a proven campaigner. An Oklahoma state senator and former member of the Oklahoma House, he had run a creditable campaign for governor in 1962. In the 1964 Senate primary, he defeated former Governor Howard Edmondson, who had appointed himself to fill Senator Kerr's vacant Senate seat. This left Fred and former Governor Raymond Gary to face each other in the run-off. Fred won.

Fred also had an excellent ad campaign. Although television was not as crucial as it would become in the following decades, it was already the principal medium of political campaigns. Ross Cummings, a local ad man who worked on Democratic races, put together a series of television spots and a print campaign to emphasize that Fred had presided over the State Senate more days than any other legislator in Oklahoma's history. "Hard Work Makes the Difference" was a winning campaign theme in this Southern populist state.

Bob and I also delved into the shadier side of politics. We bought a few votes by delivering whiskey (by 1964 Oklahoma had legalized the sale of liquor in ABC package stores) to the downtown precincts where the flophouses were. I paid for it, and he delivered it, having already made friends with the guys who ran those shelters. As far as I know, this is the only overtly illegal thing I ever did in a campaign.

One day in the headquarters Bob said, "We have been beaten like a drum in both the primary and run-off on the East Side of town." He was referring to the few streets and blocks where people of color were allowed to live and buy houses if they could afford them. Bob had numerous contacts there and was even a member of the NAACP. He looked up Clint Newton, the man who had first helped Edmondson and then Gary in their races for the nomination. Clint was a Black owner of a television-repair shop and the first real "ward healer" I had ever met. Clint was a gentleman. He heard Bob out, told him he did not need to be convinced to support the Democratic candidate against Senator Barry Goldwater, and he would not take money for his help. All he wanted was what he called a little "walking around money," which meant some gas money for himself and a few dollars for his workers.

This kind of "street money" was common in those days and still exists in some big cities. But Clint knew this election was overwhelmingly important to his constituents, who had adored John F. Kennedy. He knew they would come out in droves to support Lyndon Johnson, who was pushing for their civil rights. While at the polls, they would also vote for any Democrat that was running. Support in the Black community cost us almost nothing, and the rewards were huge. It rained on Election Day, and I spent a soggy afternoon hauling urns of coffee around in the back of my station wagon to the Black precincts. We wanted to keep everyone warm and in line if they had not voted. There were few voters, which worried me. The returns proved they had simply voted earlier in the day, just as Clint had assured us.

The county campaign was charged with just one thing: not winning but keeping Oklahoma County's winning margin under 14,000 votes. Bob drew up the campaign plan down to the last jot and tittle. We were to "make it happen." We did. Fred won, mostly because of Johnson's landslide in 1964 but also because we did our job on the ground. The Harris campaign offered me a chance to be active in the civil-rights movement, which would occupy much of my time for the next ten years. I don't know if it's because we were the last generation to grow up without television as children, but our world view was much more one of *participation* than of *observation*. We were the last generation that had the same view of patriotism as the WWII generation. It was not a personal sense of patriotism; it was decidedly a collective one. We thought of ourselves as part of the world rather than as viewers of the world. We volunteered almost obsessively. I would have an opportunity in the 1990s to be grateful to the women of my generation for their dedication.

The women I met in the civil-rights movement changed my life. For the first time I was associated with minority women who were as well educated and as affluent as I was. There were, of course, many politically involved women who were working-class wives and mothers. These were the women I met when a number of volunteers from the campaign joined to form an Oklahoma City chapter of the Panel of American Women, founded by Esther Brown of Kansas City.

Esther was instrumental in helping to bring the school-board suit in Marion, Kansas, to court. This was the Brown v. Board of Education suit that began the long court battles for equality in education. Esther was known as the "white" Brown involved in the case. She was not the Brown of Brown v. Board. Esther's idea was a good one at a time when interaction between races was minimal. She put together teams of women who were willing to go into communities and talk about their own experiences in dealing with racism and discrimination. They addressed PTAs, Rotary clubs, Kiwanis clubs, and school children in both private and public schools. Eventually the panel was organized across the country in more than sixty cities, and Esther appeared on the Phil Donohue show.

The teams were usually made up of four women. The first speaker was Jewish; the second was Roman Catholic and sometimes Hispanic; the third was African-American; and the fourth was WASP (White Anglo-Saxon Protestant). This was the first time I observed the power of having a "story." We had an impact on our audiences. Life then was still almost totally segregated, and often the Black woman on the panel was the first Black woman other than a servant many in the audience had ever seen or heard.

In the 1970s, when I was president of the National Panel of American Women, I edited two versions of these stories as I prepared a handbook for the group. These stories were filled with the accounts of witnesses to the times when a Black child's father would measure her feet with string so she could avoid the humiliation of trying to buy shoes in shops where the white salespeople were reluctant to wait on Blacks. There were stories about automobile trips across the country when Blacks could not stay in hotels or buy food in most restaurants. Black travelers in the south relied on the Green Book, a publication out of Boston produced by Victor Green. This book, published annually, listed safe homes in which to stay and restaurants that admitted Blacks in the Jim Crow south. There were few places for them that were free from harassment.

Blacks were restricted to buying houses only in certain areas in many cities. Similarly, "gentlemen's agreements" resulted in housing discrimination against Jews. And there was always the Klan's hatred against Catholics as well as memories of the bloody Tulsa race riots of 1921. But, as wives and mothers, nothing urged us on in our endeavor more than the Birmingham church bombing that killed four little girls.

●●●

Being a candidate's wife was not one of the political activities I had in mind. After my mother died in August 1965, I began to feel somewhat normal by October after all the stress. Then, one day in November, Boots came home and said he and Ted Davis had been having a drink at the Petroleum Club when they both decided to challenge the twenty-two-year incumbent congressman John Jarman. Jarman was smart enough, but he functioned simply as the tool of the *Daily Oklahoman* and the Chamber of Commerce, and he was a do-nothing congressman. In twenty-two years, he had never sponsored a major piece of legislation. He was canny enough to know that the way to stay in his seat was to keep his head down and out of the newspaper's line of fire while he voted for whatever legislation E.K. Gaylord, publisher of the *Oklahoman* and the *Chamber*, favored.

It worked. Jarman always won re-election with about 60% of the vote. But Boots and Ted thought they might be able to woo a large enough percentage of the vote from each of their respective (small) bases of support to put the Congressman in a run-off after the primary. So we ran. By now I knew something about grass-roots politics but nothing about strategy. In retrospect, I know we made every mistake in the book, but that is how you learn. At his first announcement, I should have said to Boots, "You've got to be kidding." What I did instead was throw myself into the effort. This prompted a conversation between Phil Hurst, the campaign manager, and me.

He called me one day and without preamble said, "Janet, who's going to run this campaign, you or me?" "You are,"

I answered, knowing it was the only proper and workable response. I learned to keep my mouth shut, not to talk to the press, to bite my tongue when I disagreed with a candidate's position, and to smile a lot. The *Daily Oklahoman* treated us the same way they always treated candidates they didn't favor; they ignored us. They covered only two occasions: when a candidate announced that they would run and when they lost.

The best thing that happened during the campaign occurred when Maxine Anthony came to work for our family. She sat with the children at night when we had campaign duties. Maxine was for years the hat-check girl at the Petroleum Club and remembered us from there. She was used to sleeping late and staying awake into the wee hours, a habit she never broke during the twelve years she lived with us. During the campaign, she stayed at night only when we needed her.

We lost. It took a week to count the votes. The Oklahoma County Election Board used computers for the first time, and it was a disaster. Moreover, the computers belonged to the *Daily Oklahoman*. I was enraged and convinced that the election had been stolen. Jarman got his usual 60% of the vote in nearly every precinct. In actuality, all Ted and Boots did was split the hard-core anti-Jarman vote. But thanks to Clint Newton, we did well in the Black precincts.

We raised very little outside money, so it was an expensive lesson. Oklahoma had at the time a state campaign-spending law for state primaries. The law applied even in federal elections. We were allowed to spend only $30,000 on a federal primary race, not enough money even in the 1960s to make an impact on the electorate. Everyone cheated, but I must say we did not cheat much. The primary election board meticulously went over every expenditure with me after the campaign. The result was that we were out about $30,000.

To put some perspective on the problem, four years later we sold my parents' house for $90,000.

The $30,00 cap might seem like a sufficient amount of money for a primary race for the time, but there was no effective way to use it. With no voter records on computer, phone banks had to use the telephone book, a highly inefficient method since most of the people we called were not registered and could not vote. We did not have the walk sheets or the manpower to do what we had done in the Harris campaign. We did buy what television time we could afford and used outdoor advertising. This included bumper stickers, and fence stringers (the large cardboard signs attached to "bob-wire" fences along country roads) as well as direct mail. With no newspaper coverage or free media, it would have taken easily twice the money we were able to spend legally to make an impact on the electorate. In addition, we faced an incumbent who had held office for twenty-two years.

Whenever the subject of campaign-spending limitations comes up, I think about this experience. A law that limits spending is too rigid and too hard to change. It eventually forces candidates to cheat or favors the incumbents. Imagine the ruckus that would follow if Congress were to raise the limit on the amount members could spend on their campaigns? It was hard enough for them to raise their salaries. After 1966, the Oklahoma State Legislature repealed the spending-limits law.

After we lost the primary campaign, Boots did not want to return to the law firm. Bob Kennedy, who had loyally supported us throughout the campaign, finally talked him into taking a job as head of Legal Services in Oklahoma. President Lyndon Johnson continued to support Kennedy's idea of the Peace Corps and instituted his Great Society agenda that included the War on Poverty. He began a number of programs to help the poor in the United States. The Legal Services program expanded Legal Aid, originally a private program, to make it the federally funded Legal Services. That was part of President Johnson's War on Poverty, and it was just beginning in Oklahoma City. Boots took the job and enjoyed setting up the program. His assistant was Lewis Darrell, whose wife Shirley was the daughter of Mr. J.J. Bruce, a prominent Black attorney in the city. Lew, originally from Bermuda, was a graduate of Howard University Law School.

We spent a fascinating year watching the program grow, but it was marred by one event. We went to Mexico City for a short vacation. On the way back, Boots stopped in San Antonio to consult with the people who were starting Legal Services there. He had been asked by Washington to help set up the program in other cities. I flew on to Oklahoma City. Something important happened on the airplane that I would not appreciate until years later. By this time, I was drinking more heavily than I had since college. Alcohol seemed to help me get through the many medical crises that involved my parents and deal with the strain of raising children while I was campaigning. It was about five o'clock in the evening when the stewardess asked me what I wanted to drink, and I said, "Coffee, please." Even at the time I thought that for me this was unusual.

When I landed, my parents-in-law along with my three children came to pick me up. Laudy L., my mother-in-law, slid over to allow me to drive her big Buick Roadmaster. I buckled my seat belt, but she did not. As we approached the intersection of a large boulevard, I noted that the left-turn arrow had turned yellow. I still had a green light but began to slow down, thinking that my light might change soon. There were no cars in any of our lanes. As I approached the intersection, on my left a car sped out of nowhere. I slammed on the brakes with my eyes still on the green light as the other car collided with the front of the Buick. It was a heavy car, and I was able to control it and stop before we went into the ditch that divided the highway. All that Laudy L. remembered was me yelling, "He ran the light."

Although neither car was traveling faster than about forty-five miles an hour, the Buick was totaled, and my mother-in-law was badly injured. An ambulance appeared quickly, called by a truck driver who was the first to arrive on the scene. Henry's hand was deeply gashed, and Will was under the front seat. At first, I was panicked, thinking he had been thrown from the car. Sarah and my father-in-law were not injured. The ambulance took the family to Saint Anthony's Hospital, and I stayed to talk to the police. No charges were filed, and luckily the people in the other car had only minor injuries. The driver and his companion had just left work at a manufacturing plant west of the city. They were tired after a hard day, and inattention seemed to be the cause of the crash. By God's providence, we were both sober and able to handle our vehicles as well as possible in this situation. If Laudy L. had buckled her seat belt, she would not have been injured. The police told me that if I had not buckled mine, I would have been killed.

We called Boots from the hospital, and he chartered a plane to get back to Oklahoma City. Laudy L recovered but had residual nerve damage. By sheer luck, the one surgeon in Oklahoma City who specialized in facial reconstruction and was an acquaintance of ours, happened to be in the emergency room. Boots eventually returned to San Antonio to continue his consulting. The then-Governor, John Connolly, sent an emissary to Boots's hotel to tell him "Texas don't want none of that there." Boots took the double negative to mean he could continue his work organizing Legal Services.

That fall of 1966, as Boots was working with Legal Services, I went to work on Fred Harris' second senatorial campaign. Fred had to run in 1966, only two years after he had been elected to Kerr's unexpired term. This election was for the full six years. Bob, Mary Ann Bond, and I once more staffed the Oklahoma County headquarters. We did all the state mailings and handled the distribution of bumper stickers, yard signs, and fence stringers. It was a lackluster campaign, and the Republicans fielded only nominal opposition. We won, but not by much. The results were ominous and showed a distinct erosion of Democratic support.

After the campaign, Bob and I made an analysis of the vote in Oklahoma County. Oklahoma had just elected Henry Bellmon, its first Republican governor, in the same election. We took a precinct map and Bob's slide rule, ran percentages on every precinct, and color-coded the map to show Democratic performance. What we saw from our analysis was that the blue-collar areas were beginning to vote more and more conservatively. This was especially true of the precincts in the southwest part of town near the FAA Center and the airport.

Our dear friend, Senator Mike Monroney, worked hard to get the FAA training facility built in the city. The jobs created there and at Tinker Field air base made a discernable difference in Oklahoma City's working-class neighborhoods. Everyone seemed to have a new pickup truck and a boat trailer in the driveways of their neat ranch houses. But the people who lived and worked in those areas were also moving away from the Democratic party. We sent the maps to Washington and tried to warn the senator, but he simply could not believe what was happening. Four years later Republican Henry Bellmon replaced him in the Senate.

To Bellmon's credit, the existence of the Republican party in Oklahoma was his nearly single-handed accomplishment. Earlier in the 1960s, as party chairman he had mounted a vigorous campaign to convince Oklahomans to put their party registrations where their convictions were. This ultimately redounded to his political benefit, and he surely earned every vote.

In the winter after Fred's 1966 Senate campaign, his wife LaDonna Harris asked me to help with a project. Several of us formed a committee to host the Harkness Ballet of New York, which was making a national tour to raise money for the Art Institute in Santa Fe. The Santa Fe institute trained Native American students in the arts and wanted Oklahoma City to be on the tour. Mrs. Harkness footed all the bills associated with the ballet, and our committee planned to raise money in addition to what it cost to actually produce the performance. Except for an earlier Junior League project, this was my first venture into booking a hall, selling tickets, and executing all the promotional details of mounting a performance.

It was something of an organizational disaster, but we did raise about $14,000 for scholarships, which was a paltry sum in my estimation. I felt better when I later learned that the ballet had lost money in both Houston and Los Angeles. The good news was the ballet itself; it was lovely, an original ballet taken from Hopi legends. As a bonus, I got to know Lee Udall, wife of Stuart Udall, who was Interior Secretary during both the Kennedy and Johnson administrations. Lee was a truly lovely person, and later, after we moved to Virginia, she and I spent a couple of years carpooling our children.

After my experience with the committee to host the Harkness Ballet, I put some of my newfound knowledge to work on a committee that was producing another new ballet, the Four Moons, that featured the great ballerinas from Oklahoma. The idea originated, I believe, with either the retired prima ballerina Yvonne Chouteau, who was teaching ballet at the University of Oklahoma along with her husband, Miguel Terekhov, or with Moscelyne Larkin of the Tulsa ballet company. She was another Native American ballerina and was teaching with her husband Roman Jasinski. They combined forces to persuade Rosella Hightower to come from France and Marjorie Tallchief to come from Chicago, to dance together. The ballet was originally planned to be Five Moons, but Maria Tallchief was unable to join her sister for the performance. Even though all the dancers were considered past their prime, it was a stunning evening. We did one performance in Tulsa and another in Oklahoma City.

Along with all my arts committee involvement, I continued my political activity. I was asked to be Fifth District Chair for the Democratic Party. Bob Kennedy engineered the deal. Jarman, as the District's Congressman, graciously said he would not object to my appointment. Those were the "bad old" party days. Running a political party was an inside job. The entire state party apparatus consisted of fourteen of us who ran the state party. The "reforms" of the McGovern era in the 1970s would strip the parties of their power to nominate and would dilute their influence on politics in general.

One experience stands out during that year. Senators Robert F. Kennedy and Hubert Humphrey showed up in Oklahoma City. Fred Harris, a good friend to both, had talked them into coming to Oklahoma. Humphrey spoke somewhere the day before Kennedy arrived in the city. We sat in the Presidential Suite in the old Biltmore Hotel in downtown Oklahoma City, visiting with the loquacious vice president while the secret service tended bar and hovered around. The only problem was that we had to get Humphrey out of the hotel and onto his Air Force Two plane so we could clean up the suite for Kennedy's arrival. We barely made it.

Boots, Bob Kennedy, and I then went to the airport with the Harrises to meet Robert Kennedy. Boots was the designated driver, and he also ran interference for Kennedy through the crowds at the airport. The evening paper had a picture of Boots shoving people aside so Kennedy could get on the escalator at the airport. The next morning, we went to the hotel early to have breakfast with Kennedy, the Harrises, and a few of our friends. I remember exactly what I wore; it was a black sleeveless wool dress with camel trim and a long camel coat. Their style evoked the one made popular by Jacqueline Kennedy. I wore a gold pin shaped like a bull (to evoke Taurus, my zodiac sign), and below it was a PT 109 campaign pin left over from the 1960 campaign. Robert Kennedy teased me about having all my bases covered—the PT boat pin for Kennedy, and the bull for Johnson.

I sat next to Kennedy on the ride to Norman. For once in my life I was completely speechless. Our own station wagon was the transportation vehicle, and I was so awestruck that I didn't say a word all the way down and back. The evening newspaper had a picture of me sitting next to Robert Kennedy in the back of the car. I have always considered it to be seven and a half minutes of my fifteen minutes of fame allotted to everyone by Andy Warhol.

Kennedy was to make a speech in Norman at the University of Oklahoma. His topic was farm policy, but I don't remember anything he said, only his speech pattern with its halting delivery and Massachusetts flavor. The students applauded loudly and crowded around the car as we left, making progress slow indeed. On the way back to the city, Kennedy asked for a pen. He wrote a note to Boots on the front page of the paper next to the picture of the two of them taken at the airport. I remember that the trees were just leafing out and that the sere Oklahoma landscape was beginning to come alive. There was a feeling of hope.

Chapter 13

VIRGINIA

THE SUMMER OF 1967 began pleasantly. Sarah went to camp in Wisconsin, and I took her to Chicago on our way. We had a wonderful couple of days looking around, going to the planetarium and museums and then to a restaurant called the Kingsholm. It offered a Swedish smorgasbord and had a theater with a puppet show. We saw "Kismet." In late July, Boots, the boys, and I went to our vacation home in Wisconsin where Sarah joined us. By this time, the newspapers were full of stories about the race riots taking place in Detroit. I was still involved with the Panel of American Women, and by this time I was a member of the NAACP. We were deeply disturbed as one city after another erupted in violence.

In the middle of August, I took the children home from Wisconsin on the train to allow Boots to drive the station wagon home and return to work. Milwaukee was one of the US cities experiencing race riots. As we went through that city on the train, afraid of random shooting, I made the children kneel on the floor and look out of the window. The streets were littered with debris, but they appeared to be empty except for armed National Guardsmen.

Boots and his parents met us at the station when we arrived in Oklahoma City. He asked me to ride with him and let the children ride with their grandparents.

"What would you think about moving to Washington, DC?" he asked as we drove.

"When?"

"Now. Fred called and offered me a job on the staff of the commission studying the riots."

"When would you go?"

"Monday."

I protested. Monday was the day our seven-year-old, Henry, was scheduled to have corrective surgery for the bones in his legs. It was a serious operation that involved cutting the femur and rotating and then pinning the bone. It was like having two broken legs, and he would be in a body cast for at least six weeks. I asked Boots if he could wait to go until Wednesday. He said he could not, so he flew to Washington and I went to the hospital. My mother-in-law, Laudys L, kept me company during the operation. It was awful, and after it Henry was in excruciating pain. Finally, the drugs put him to sleep, and I went home. Maxine, who by now had almost become our de facto au pair, was with Will and Sarah. I walked into the house, took a bottle of Scotch from the bar and headed for the bedroom. It was the first time I remember being alone and making a conscious decision to get dead drunk. It would happen often in the future.

Henry survived, I survived, and we both adjusted to all the things the doctor and his office had forgotten to tell us. We had not been informed that he would be in a body cast for more than two months, would miss a semester of school, and would have to learn to walk again, all of which was very painful. Boots rented a house in McLean, Virginia, near the Harrises. In late August I flew with Sarah to Washington where she started fifth grade at Churchill Road School. She and Boots lived at the Jefferson Hotel, and I returned to Oklahoma City. Boots drove Sarah to McLean to school each day. She stayed with our friends Betty and Bill McCandless until her father could take her back to the hotel in the evenings. Bill McCandless was Fred Harris' state campaign manager and an excellent businessman. He came to Washington as the director of the Ozarka Regional Commission, one of the many poverty programs created by President Johnson.

Sometime in October, I closed the Oklahoma City house and drove Will and our au pair Maxine to Washington. Allied Van Lines brought our furniture, and I set up the McLean house. I left them and went back to be with Henry, who had stayed with his Aunt Marilyn. Finally, when he was out of his body cast, he and I flew to Washington. I felt like a mother cat with a litter of kittens as I moved them from one place to another, one kitten at a time. Fortunately for us, Maxine's son Scotty had just joined the Navy. He left college to do this, which aggravated his mother. As it happened, he continued his education in the Navy, but his absence from Oklahoma City convinced Maxine that she might as well leave and see something of the world with us. She stayed with us for twelve years.

Boots's involvement on the staff of the Commission on Civil Disorder was all-consuming. He helped to research and write the report. Reading it today reveals how far we have come and how little we have progressed. The language of the report is formal and precise. It is interesting to note that in the report Black people were referred to as "Negros." The Black is Beautiful movement would come later. The most outstanding part of the report was its accuracy in stating what sparked the riots and describing the involvement of the police in them. The suggestions the report makes for remediation are the same as the ones being made today; they have never been implemented. When the report was issued, President Johnson, who was still running for president, had little to say, since the report was brutally honest about the mistakes made by both federal and state officials. Like so many governmental reports, it gathers dust on library shelves.

For the first two years we spent in Virginia, I did almost nothing but be a mom, take an interest in Boots' work, and assist LaDonna Harris with various projects. I hid from the Junior League until they found me and said, "Either sign up or ship out." The League in Washington was completely different then from the Oklahoma City League in which I had been a member. The Washington League was big, active, and for its time, diverse. Many of the women were employed, and the League accepted Jewish members. The projects the League chose to support were timely. I spent one year working in the racially mixed Adams Morgan section of Washington and part of a year with a Police Community Relations project in the city's Northeast. One of the things I did there was to ride around in a DC squad car as part of a program designed to familiarize civic leaders with what the police did daily.

The final two years of the 1960s marked another profound change in America. This one, unlike the transition from the 1950s, was apparent, violent, and vocal. The anti-war protests were in full swing. Boots got a nose full of tear gas when he was sharing an office on R Street in 1969. What I remember most vividly were the young people who marched from the Pentagon's parking lot across Memorial Bridge and went on to the Capitol. I drove down the parkway one evening just to watch the seemingly endless stream of people carrying candles in the dusk. Each of them was reported to be wearing a bracelet with the name of a United States service member killed in Vietnam.

My life was exciting and pleasant. I spent a good deal of time on Capitol Hill when there was legislation of interest to me. At a birthday party for Fred, I performed a song-and-dance tribute with Betty McCandless and the wife of his chief of staff. The party took place in one of the large committee rooms of the Old Senate Office Building. I looked up in the middle of the routine, and there was Vice President Humphrey, laughing along with everyone else. Luckily the jolly man understood and appreciated our corny presentation.

Our relations with the Harrises became strained in the spring of 1968. They enthusiastically supported Hubert Humphry for president, while I prepared to go to the '69 convention as a Robert Kennedy delegate. I was still fifth district co-chair in Oklahoma since we planned to return to Oklahoma City after the Kerner Commission Report was finished.

As it happened, I did not attend the convention. We were becoming fixed in the Washington area, and the district chair challenged me, asking if I wasn't really staying in office to be able to go to the convention. In fact, I was, and I told him so. I said I would resign on one condition—that I could name the person who would take my seat. I named Clint Newton, and the chair agreed with my choice. I never knew if he kept his part of the bargain.

In the spring of 1968 Fred Harris and Walter Mondale were asked to chair the Senatorial Campaign Committee's annual fundraising dinner. The date for the dinner was April 4. The committee staff does the work of putting on the affair, but they ask the wives of the Senators to participate. In turn the wives often designate their liaison. LaDonna Harris asked me and Joan Mondale asked her friend Nancy Black. We did our minor parts.

The evening of the dinner, Fred called and asked us to pick up Nancy Dickerson. We did not know them, but the Dickersons lived in the neighborhood across Chain Bridge Road in McLean and their boys came over to play with the boys in our neighborhood.

We picked up Nancy, drove to the Washington Hilton, and went directly to the VIP reception. Nancy Dickerson sailed right in, and we were stopped at the door. The staff had neglected to get our Social Security numbers for the Secret Service. The same thing happened to the Blacks, so the four of us stood outside, occasionally waving to friends and having short conversations at the open door as the Secret Service looked on. We could not tell what was going on but the atmosphere in the reception decidedly changed. Then there was a hush and someone on the loudspeaker said, "Ladies and gentlemen, the Vice President will not be speaking, and the dinner is cancelled. We have received word the Rev. Martin Luther King has been shot and killed."

The Harrises and the Mondales joined us in the hallway and with nothing more to do, we went to the Mondales' for a drink. I don't remember much of the evening. We were in such shock. Fritz tended bar, but we were not in the mood for conversation. Their home was a few blocks from the National Cathedral, and the tolling of the great Bourdon Bell filled the silence. Finally, we simply went home.

The next day I flew out to Oklahoma for a Democratic Committee Meeting. Northeast Washington DC had exploded in fear, frustration, and rioting. Great plumes of smoke rose and drifted to the east.

I made a rather incoherent speech to the Democratic ladies and spent a lot of my time that evening with my Black friends in the hotel bar.

Then tragedy struck again. In June, Robert Kennedy was killed. Boots and I were watching television late at night, waiting to hear what Kennedy would say after his victory in California. In shocked disbelief I watched the scene in the hotel kitchen. Robert Kennedy was lying inert on the floor, his eyes fixed on nothing. The first thing I did the morning after Kennedy was killed was to call the Harrises and invite them to dinner. They had lost a colleague and a personal friend. We had lost what we really thought was the last hope for our generation to make a difference. Eating with friends seemed to be the only constructive thing to do at the time. So we chewed on sirloin and ate Caesar salad and baked potatoes.

Other than the dinner the night Dr. King was killed we had seen little of the Harrises. They were supporting Hubert Humphrey while we supported Robert Kennedy. We put our whole-hearted support behind Hubert Humphrey. I continued my political activity, and helped in a very small way with the Humphrey campaign. The only other thing of note was helping LaDonna Harris with a conference initiated by President Johnson called Women in the War Against Poverty. It was a great success, and it began my long friendship with Mildred Robbins Leet, who, with her second husband Glen, later founded the Trickle Up Program. This program has helped thousands of women, the poorest of the poor, start projects and small businesses around the world. Mildred and Glen were a remarkable couple.

In June of 1968 we went to Wisconsin to a new location. In the spring my brother sold the lake house where we had spent our childhood summers to our lakeside neighbors the Hutchinsons. They, in turn, called us to see if we would like to buy their small cottage. Since it was all we could afford and because we could be at the lake for only a few weeks a year, we took their offer. We split the extra lot between the two houses that my father had purchased when my parents had built their house. This would be the first summer we would spend at the small cabin we called the Lake House.

Before we left Washington we put our furniture in storage, thinking we might spend both summer and winter in

Wisconsin instead of returning to Oklahoma City. Almost as soon as we arrived in Wisconsin, Secretary of Interior Stewart Udall called. He asked Boots to become Associate Solicitor for Indian Affairs.

"What can I do in six months?" Boots asked, knowing that whether Humphrey or Nixon won, there would be a change of administration and personnel. "Please," Stewart said, "there is a lot I want to accomplish for the Indian people before I leave, and I need your help." How could Boots refuse? We returned to Washington; rented a house in McLean, Virginia, around the corner from our previous rental; and moved in—Boots, kids, Maxine, a stray cat, and me.

It was a hard year for me. Boots was gone a lot, still speaking around the country about the Kerner Commission Report, and he often needed to travel for his work at the Interior Department. I drank a lot when he was home and more than usual when he was gone. I just barely took care of the children. That spring, as I sat on the bed with a terrific hangover, I called Alcoholics Anonymous. It was the first time I admitted to myself that once I took a drink I was beyond control. I called the AA Intergroup Office, and the person on the other end of the line did not ask me for my phone number or name or even offer much information. I probably didn't sound very receptive, and I didn't follow up.

Nixon won the election in the fall. That spring, we bought a house on Merrie Ridge Road in McLean, Virginia, and decided to stay in Washington. By the end of 1969 my life and my world had changed more than I could have imagined. A decade that had started with such promise ended in utter loss—both the Kennedys and Dr. King were dead, along with our dreams of making a difference. The young people who were making headlines and noise were not of our generation. After all, they were the ones who said, "never trust anyone over thirty." We were just over thirty. It was as though we were standing in the middle of an enormous storm, shouting into the wind. The WWII generation was firmly in charge of public policy and not much interested in our "new" ideas, and the kids just younger than us could not care less about the suggestions we made. I was astounded at the far left's mistrust of government. This mistrust would grow and would push the far left not just to campus unrest but to the origin of the Weathermen. Even though there was a great deal of public pressure against the far left, their anti-government stance became embedded in public discourse and was exacerbated by the Vietnam War. My generation looked on government as the only trustworthy safety net. The post-war generation's mistrust would soon be the prevailing attitude.

I have a surreal memory from those years of walking down First Street in Oklahoma City with LaDonna Harris. For some reason we were there together sometime in the late 1960s. We were talking about these changing attitudes, and I had the actual impression that the world was shifting under my feet. It would take the grinding 1970s to solidify the changes begun in the 1960s.

Silent or not, my generation changed the world in several ways. We led the Women's Movement, and we participated wholeheartedly in the Civil Rights Movement. Martin Luther King, born in 1929, was really one of us. Perhaps our most lasting triumph was another legacy of John Kennedy's vision and Johnson's power, the NASA program and its astronauts who were just our age. On Christmas 1968, Sarah and I went to the National Cathedral for a midnight service, acutely aware of the small object and its human cargo that was circling the earth. And in the summer of 1969, our generation landed on the moon.

Chapter 14

THE HOUSE IN MCLEAN

THE CHILDREN WERE growing up. In the 1970s they finished elementary school in McLean. All three of them attended Cooper Junior High School in the seventh and eighth grades, and then the boys went on to Langley High School. Sarah, a shy young woman, expressed a desire to go to private school. She and I went to National Cathedral School and Madeira, both in McLean, to talk to admissions faculty.

I wanted the decision to be entirely hers. I preferred National Cathedral simply because I loved the Gothic buildings and the Cathedral Close surrounding them. But after the interviews, I knew her choice would be Madeira. She had not taken algebra I in the eighth grade, and she was worried about the omission. Math had never been her strongest subject, although overall she was an excellent student with excellent grades.

The response of the admissions interviewer at National Cathedral was somewhat deprecating. She said they often had new students with such a lack and assured Sarah that they had remedial classes for them. But at Madeira, Barbara Boerner, the head of admissions, looked at her and said,

"Good. The quality of middle school algebra varies so much we would just as soon our students started fresh." That settled Sarah's decision; she attended Madeira as a day student. And Madeira had horses, a major plus for her.

The school showed her a wide world. Madeira had release time every Wednesday, when the young women worked during the day at a job somewhere in the Washington area. For two years Sarah was an aide in a District of Columbia elementary school. During her junior year, Boots got her a job as an intern in Speaker Carl Albert's office. The speaker was from Oklahoma and had known Boots's father. Mr. Albert saw to it that Sarah was treated like family in the office. In addition, she worked there during the Watergate affair, which proved doubly interesting. She was in the office the day Vice President Spiro Agnew resigned and his letter was delivered to the speaker's office. Somehow the original letter was lost, but she retained a photocopy of it as a memento.

The boys pursued their own interests. For Henry it was theater, and for Will it was sports. Each of them had a large and close group of friends. They and their gang of friends were all good boys but got into just the kinds of scrapes high-school boys seem unable or unwilling to avoid. Both of them made forays with their friends to the famed bar The Tombs in Georgetown where, I am told, beer was drunk.

One midnight we received a visit from the Fairfax County Police that involved the destruction of a mailbox. It turned out that one of Henry's best friends had broken up with his girlfriend and was unhappy enough to blow up her family's mailbox. Henry was driving the car and therefore was considered to be an accomplice.

I awoke sometime after midnight to the flashing of a police car's lights. I panicked; my first thought was that there had been a car accident. As I tossed on a robe and walked out of the bedroom, Henry emerged from his room and said, "I think that's for me, Mom." I was so relieved to see him that what followed seemed immaterial. Officer Green of the county police force handled the issue masterfully. He was calm and dead-on honest about what the kids had done and its implications. There was no doubt that reparations had to be made. He also received complete cooperation from the parents involved. The boys spent four Saturdays working around the house of the man who owned the splintered mailbox.

It took me fifty years to learn about Will's exploits. One that involved a rock-climbing adventure at a quarry gave me chills. Another was his brush with the police, much less dramatic than Henry's. Apparently, the group of teenage boys decided to indulge in that short-lived fad of the '70s, "streaking." The gang, in full streaking mode, failed to see the cop car in the neighborhood. When the car flashed its lights, the boys ran for home. Most of the time spent at our house on Merrie Ridge Road was normal with its basic family doings, and we had our wonderful dog Jeannie, half beagle and half dachshund and totally lovable.

My mother-in-law Laudys L died in the summer of 1971. She had a heart attack, and Boots flew from Wisconsin to Oklahoma to be with her. Sarah, her favorite grandchild, also went with her dad and had a visit with her grandmother. Like my father, Laudys L continued to recuperate and seemed to be fine, but then she suddenly died following another attack. After my mother-in-law's death, we took my father-in-law with us for a short vacation at the lake. Then we drove from Wisconsin to Oklahoma City and spent two weeks closing the Taliaferros' house and shipping its furniture to Virginia. We drove both our station wagon and the Taliaferros' Buick back to Virginia through the Tennessee mountains. It had been a sad summer, but everyone seemed to enjoy the trip. Sarah loved Asheville,

North Carolina, and the Biltmore (on the Vanderbilt Estate). The boys loved Gatlinburg, which was halfway between quaint and Las Vegas.

My father-in-law lived with us for about two years. The children in his neighborhood had dubbed him "Mr. Boots," and it stuck with us to determine which Henry B. "Boots" Taliaferro we were talking about.

Mr. Boots was legally blind but got on very well. He could maneuver around in our cabin in Wisconsin and our house in Virginia. He and our dog Jeannie took a daily walk. His eyes were just good enough to see the white sidewalk, so he kept up his daily routine of walking nearly two miles when the weather was pleasant. He and I spent quite a bit of time together. The only disagreement we had was over the Vietnam War. As a World War I veteran, he was livid over the war's protesters. I disapproved of the war, but my focus was on the civil-rights movement, so I wasn't protesting.

These were the years of bell-bottom trousers and long hair. The men tried Nehru jackets, and casual dressing came into fashion. The women tried miniskirts and hot pants. Food was changing, and all kinds of foreign foods and ingredients began to be available in Washington. When we first moved there, Washington had a few good French restaurants. There was one Indian restaurant near Dupont Circle in what looked like a former house of ill repute. I prepared Mexican food at home until I met Lynda and Chuck Robb and discovered Speedy Gonzales, a hole-in-the-wall that Lady Bird Johnson had ferreted out. Speedy's was run by a family, and the cooking was good ol' Texas style. Everything was served on paper plates with plastic forks and paper napkins. The place occupied two rather derelict houses, only one of which had a liquor license, so if you wanted beer with your food, you had to wait to get into that one. Speedy and his family opened a place on Capitol Hill in the 1970s.

Life was tranquil, but it was interrupted by more trips to the hospital than I could wish. Henry had his fourth operation (fifth, if I count his tonsillectomy). In the meantime, I had a gland in my jaw opened up and then had a hysterectomy about two weeks before Henry's hospital stays began. I ran into John Walsh, my surgeon, when Henry was in the operating room. "What have you done, moved in?" John teased me. By this time, Henry and I were old hands at all of this. I found the linen closet in the ward and usually changed his sheets and bathed him. "Are you a nurse?" one of the RNs asked. I said I was not, but Boots insisted I lied.

Henry had his own stethoscope, which the interns kept carrying off. Finally, someone permanently pinched it. We would drive by the hospital, and Henry would muse, "Wonder who has my stethoscope?" I had bought it; I knew it was cheap imitation and hoped it did not jeopardize anyone's life. I wasn't sure what could really be heard through it.

Meanwhile, Boots's career was changing rapidly. He left the Department of Interior in the spring of 1969 after the transition period following Richard Nixon's inauguration. In Boots's view and from what he heard from people who had been in the department a long time, some of them since the Roosevelt administration, this was a different sort of transition. The sacking of people in the department was wholesale and even included Republicans, some of whom had long tenure. The lines of authority and communication were set up at the assistant-secretary level; they bypassed the secretary level and went straight to the White House.

An effective president of the United States must understand at least one of two things: how the government really works, and how the people of the United States really think and behave. Johnson and Nixon both knew exactly how the government worked. Both had been Senators when the US Senate had great talent and great power. Johnson's style was one of inclusion. If he needed the help of someone on Capitol Hill, he picked up the phone. He relied on his vast knowledge of the place and its people and applied pressure where and when it was needed to achieve his ends. From his few encounters with Johnson, Boots concluded that the president was more adept at invading someone's personal space than anyone he had ever met. A big man, Johnson gave new meaning to "leaning on" someone.

Nixon's style was one of paranoid exclusivity. The result was a fiefdom that probably came as close to being a coup that we thought this country would ever see. Even long-time Republican Senators were aghast at how thoroughly they were ignored. One complained to Boots that the White House would not even answer his phone calls. These excesses eventually led to Watergate and the threat of President Nixon's impeachment. Rather than face the threat he resigned, and many of us breathed a sigh of relief that so trustworthy a person as Gerald Ford would take over the presidency.

Nixon's administration was not all bad, although it was thoroughly cynical. I must remind myself that the Environmental Protection Agency was started under his administration. In addition, there were significant changes to our monetary system. The Nixon administration was also responsible for the great foreign policy step of the decade, the opening of trade with China. Nixon's accomplishment was rivaled only by Jimmy Carter's efforts at Camp David to settle the Middle East disputes. However, Nixon had earlier been merciless to those who had previously suggested we deal with a government that represents the largest communist population on the face of the earth. Nevertheless, he was the one to open the door to China.

However, too many of us remembered Richard Nixon and his ugly campaign against Helen Gahagan Douglas when Nixon was first elected to Congress. He was a terrible red-baiter, and he accused the Congresswoman of being so "pink" that even her underwear was pink. The slur was demeaning, and the charges were baseless. Nixon had been in the Congress all through the McCarthy Era, and he continued to bash anyone he considered a communist or a communist sympathizer. He was proud of his rather tasteless confrontation with Russian Premier Khrushchev.

Around this time, our neighbor Murray Chotiner, who had been teaching law at Howard University, tragically died as the result of a minor car accident on Georgetown Pike. Like so many officeholders under Nixon, he had done something to displease the president and had been banished. Nixon's treatment of Murray had evidently been egregious, since it was the subject of a particularly blunt eulogy by the rabbi at his funeral service. I attended the services at the Temple B'nai Israel with Admiral and Mrs. Clarence Hill, who lived across the street from us in McLean. President and Mrs. Nixon sat in the front row. I was seated on the aisle, and as the president passed me, my overwhelming impression was that he looked as if he were wearing not his own face but one of the rubber masks of himself that were sold in the shops of Washington.

During this time, Boots shared offices with Abe and Lefty Weisbrodt, who had an active practice representing Native American tribes. Rich Allan, who had left Interior at the end of the Johnson administration, had gone to work for their firm. Rich and Dorothy Allan became particularly close friends of ours. Business was sparse, but Boots was still occasionally asked to speak about the Commission on Civil Disorder. The Weisbrodt association gave him a chance to practice some Indian law, which had been part of his training at the University of Oklahoma. Boots tried one of the final cases to appear before the Indian Claims Commission. The case was brought by the Joseph Band of the Nez Perce tribe. The Nez

Perce sued the government for reparations due to the tribe's forceful removal in 1877 from its traditional homelands in northeast Oregon to a reservation in Idaho. Their resistance to their removal by the US Army was professional and effective. The incident was known as the Nez Perce War. Joseph was the principal chief of the tribe. Eventually he led a group of this tribe, known as the Joseph Band, on a desperate run for the Canadian border where they could be free of US domination and where several tribes had resettled. The Joseph Band fought a rearguard defense all the way and came to nearly forty miles of the Canadian border. Chief Joseph's eloquent speech when he surrendered remains an example of grace under fire. Boots argued the case as an incidence of genocide. He didn't win, but he did get a split decision when one of the three judges ruled in his favor.

After two years with the Weisbrodt association, Boots moved to his own offices and was associated with Casey, Lane, and Mittendorff, the New York firm in which he worked as a senior partner until 1979. He was the Washington-based partner for the firm, in which he continued his work on Indian affairs and represented the Klinget and Haida tribes in their successful suits for reparations. He also worked in oil, gas, and pipeline matters and became involved with the South African Sugar Association.

Boots was skeptical of representing white South African business at the height of that country's apartheid. The first time we took clients from South Africa out to dinner we agonized, "But what will we talk about?" However, we found the people he represented were delightful. Most of the sugar people were British South Africans and were more liberal than their Dutch counterparts. We found them eager to talk about race relations. However, it was like talking to people from the 1950s. Their hearts were in the right place, but they seemed hopelessly naïve about the situation. Yet, as time proved, when apartheid was finally overthrown, Bishop Tutu and President Mandela relied on the goodwill of such white South Africans.

●●●

Along with my political activity in the 1970s, I continued to be involved in the community, doing most of my Junior League work as a docent at the National Gallery of Art. This was a gratifying experience; not only did I learn a great deal more about art history, which had been my college minor, but I was able to work with school children and introduce them to the joys of looking at paintings. Still, my primary interests in life were Democratic politics and civil rights. I saw injustice and the poverty that had surrounded me as a child, and I wanted to "fix" it.

I also continued to be active with the Panel of American Women and served as its national president. We struggled to make a meaningful contribution to the civil-rights dialogue. Two things stood in the way of our progress. The first was the waning interest in the racial struggle; people were instead talking about "ethnicity" and "cultural heritage." Although important, these things paled in our minds as we focused on the injustices suffered by racial minorities in the United States since the country's origin. We always tried to present the ideals of universal suffrage and the opportunity for any man or woman to pursue whatever were their personal goals in education, employment, or housing. We stayed true to our purpose. We were particularly aware of what we called "institutional racism." Individuals seemed to be more easily persuaded than corporations.

The second impediment to the Panel's growth was more serious. We could not come to any agreement as to how to sustain our activities as an organization. Oddly, we could discuss any phase of society that was dominated by a group in control. Of course, most of these institutional groups were made up of white males, most of whom were from the World War II generation. We could see this, discuss it, parse it, and condemn it, but we could never fully understand our part in it.

The National Panel of American Women was undone by its inability to understand its own feminine point of view. Quite simply, the organization could never accept the burden of having to raise money to pay its own way. There were passionate arguments about how what we were doing was all-volunteer and should be above money grubbing. The few men on the board patiently explained it took money to run any organization, especially one that functioned in some sixty cities across the United States. They emphasized there was no such thing in business as a free lunch.

The women of the organization could not accept this. They wanted to rely on the hard-working core of women in Kansas City who slaved to raise the money to keep the national office open, provide printed materials, perform public relations, and keep in touch with everybody. We finally wore out this dedicated group. We had a huge national meeting under my leadership and moderated by Jonathan Cook, the head of a group in Washington called the Support Center. Their specific mission was to help nonprofit organizations that had governance problems. Jonathan and I, along with my board, struggled for three days to arrive at some consensus among the panel members about how the organization should proceed. The lack of success was manifest in the remark of the frustrated parliamentarian we had hired for the marathon. Near the end of the final day she said, "I have never worked with a group before who could not even agree on classes of membership."

The organization continued into the late 1970s. It still maintained an office and did programs in Kansas City, but it really ceased to be a national organization after Linda May from Houston became president. Linda was a wonderful president and did one outstanding thing for us by arranging a reception to honor the Panel of American Women at the White House. We met in the Roosevelt room, often called the "fish room" because pictures of fish had been hung on the walls before some Roosevelt portraits were moved there. The room was in the West Wing, and it was a special occasion. I do not remember which staff member met with us, but that wasn't important. We celebrated among ourselves our own success in carrying the message of equality.

At the last minute, I bought a Jefferson Cup inscribed for Linda, because I knew the group well enough to know they would never think of presenting our president with a token of appreciation. Such tokens were always taken care of by our faithful Executive Secretary Shirley Morantz, who had finally succumbed to burnout. I gave the cup to Linda at the White House and was immediately berated by a couple of the board members because I made the presentation on behalf of the organization without consulting the board. They were right, but by then I was accustomed to being autocratic about several things. I recall one of the more poignant moments when the Panel of American Women held a training session in Rochester, New York. There was a lull in the activity, and one young woman stared off into space and remarked, "Do you remember when we were going to eliminate racism?"

One of my many trips to Kansas City for the panel resulted in a terrifying experience. I had been at the panel's office, meeting with the staff and with a young woman from New York City. She had written a book about working-class women and was doing some research with us. After the meetings, we went to dinner in a suburban restaurant with a few of the Kansas City women. After dinner about four of us stopped at a booth in the bar to have a nightcap. Just before the eleven o'clock closing time, a thin man wearing a ski mask came in waving a gun. He appeared to be very young and was trembling. He ordered us to get up and follow him. It was just before Halloween, and a man at another table said something like "Hey, man, you can't be serious."

There was a loud explosion near my right ear. I was sure he was shooting blanks because I heard nothing whiz past my ear the way it happens in the movies. All of us dutifully got up and followed the masked man. My mind seemed completely disassociated from my body. I walked along carefully, looking for any chance to escape, but knew that any such idea was foolish. He herded us to the walk-in refrigerator. The son of the owner fumbled with the lock and got it off the door. The lock itself suddenly disappeared, probably into a vat of chicken salad.

The masked guy closed the door, but he could not lock us in. The owner's son said, "Just be still. Don't say or do anything." After a short while the phone began to ring. It rang for a long time, and still we waited. Finally, the police opened the refrigerator door. The owner had been the one who called. His son told us that he called every evening when the place was to be closed just to be sure everything was all right. After getting no answer, he had immediately summoned the police.

Our guest from New York and I had left our purses, our money, and our airline tickets in the booth. Luckily, the thief had taken only the money from the cash registers. The police questioned us, and I told them about the "blank" the robber had fired. "Oh, yes," the policeman said as he got up and dug a bullet out of the wall over my right shoulder. Next, they asked our guest to identify herself. She did, and then said in a shaking voice, "I was born and raised in New York City and nothing like this has *ever* happened to me before."

If the Panel of American Women had not learned a lesson as a group about feminine dependence, it seemed that many of the panelists as individuals had got the message. I was deeply impressed when I later moved back to Oklahoma City in the 1980s to see at a luncheon that every woman there had gone on from her experience as a panelist to become involved in the community in some professional capacity. Many had advanced degrees, and all of them held some sort of paid position. I found a similar thing with Washington-area former panelists. They held responsible jobs and even elective office after becoming long-time members of the Fairfax County Board of Supervisors. The Panel had been a great training ground for us, and I believe we had done some lasting good in the community at large.

Chapter 15

THE BUSINESS OF CAMPAIGNS

MY REAL LESSONS in independence were delivered through my political activity. Once we were established in the Washington area and had decided to stay there indefinitely, I began to be active once more in Democratic politics. I worked as a minor volunteer in the Humphrey-Muskie campaign clipping newspapers. In the 1970s I helped to sell trinkets to raise money for the campaign. That was in 1972, the great watershed presidential election year that witnessed the egregious mishandling of money by the Nixon campaign and then the Watergate scandal and the passage of the Federal Election Commission Act of 1974. I acted as treasurer for the boutique, and it was interesting to be around the finance office of the Muskie campaign also. One day as I was on the way there, the volunteer coordinator for the campaign stopped me and said "You know how to do a get-out-the-vote operation. We need you in Milwaukee." I agreed to go.

Sarah was on spring break from Madeira and went with me to Wisconsin for the primary. My job was to help with the get-out-the-vote (or GOTV) effort. I found myself among a flock of young volunteers, most of whom had no idea what to do. There were a few experienced campaigners present but not many. Several of the young people were students at the University of Oklahoma's School of Law. One very bright Oklahoma law student pulled me aside the first day. "What's a CD?" she whispered to me. "Congressional District," I whispered back.

The students weren't the only ones in Wisconsin who had Oklahoma connections. Pam Fleischaker was also in Milwaukee. She was co-chair of the Muskie effort there; she had little campaign experience, but did have an extensive background in press and national issues. All of us engaged in an all-out effort. I pulled together the rudiments of an attempt to cover the polls and distribute literature for election day. I was assisted by the girlfriend of one of the young men. She had experience and flew in for the last few days. Although having such a partner was helpful, we lost decisively. The bad press Muskie had at the beginning of his campaign did its damage, but—at least in Wisconsin—it was Governor George Wallace who made the difference. By the time I reached Milwaukee, the extensive phone banks showed that Muskie's support was melting away. Wallace's hard populist and racist appeal was the major factor in Muskie's loss there. I was appalled that working-class voters in the North were attracted to him. In later years I would come to appreciate what drove that shift. The Democratic Party blew itself up with the busing controversy.

After the passing of Brown v. Board in 1954 integration of universities was not without protest, but it was the integration of elementary and high school that drew the fire. It caused Virginia to implement "massive resistance" and to force President Eisenhower to invoke the Insurrection Act, sending troops in to integrate nine students in Little Rock High School. Opposition to integration erupted in city after city for twenty years. It gave governors such as Orville Faubus and George Wallace a platform. It affected cities as different as Boston, Massachusetts, and Charlotte, North Carolina. Busing was considered by many citizens to be an example of overreach by Democrats. Arguably, school integration was the prime reason the Democratic Party was stamped "elitist," alienating blocs of its base and throwing the door wide open to the Republican Party's Southern Strategy. Parents unhappy with government fooling about with their children sought various remedies such as home schooling and a flight to "heritage" private schools.

Fooling with people's kids was a loser in politics. Ultimately, forced desegregation made no sense even though at the time it appeared necessary. Oklahoma City was a case in point.

Around the time that Oklahoma City became "integrated," I remember having a conversation with Bill Carmack, who was head of the communications department at the University of Oklahoma. He headed the committee to plan Oklahoma City's school integration. "Bill," I protested at the time, "you don't know what you have done. You are busing kids from northeast to northwest. It won't work in this town." The result was white flight to private "heritage" schools. In addition, our Black panelists in Oklahoma City along with some white families had established themselves in an enclave in the northeast part of the city. Their support for the local school made it a model public school. Then their kids were suddenly bused off to another school. George Wallace's campaign signs on every city bus told the story.

For me, the trip to Milwaukee to campaign was revealing in another way. I quickly decided not to be involved at the presidential level ever again. My preference was always for Congressional races. They were small enough to be intimate and important enough to allow you to raise the sort of money needed for a campaign. But I would not have missed the Wisconsin primary. I made life-long friends and learned a lot, and I think I may also have taught a lot. In the plane on the way back to Washington, Sarah said, "Gosh, I had friends going on spring break to Florida, Europe, and the Caribbean. I went to Milwaukee."

In July, Boots and I went with LaDonna and Fred Harris to the Democratic Convention in Miami. It was just as heartbreaking in some ways as the 1968 debacle in Chicago. "Party reform" had taken over, and the floor was filled with McGovern followers, most of whom were as inexperienced as the people I had met in Milwaukee. The volunteers meant well, but the McGovern campaign appeared to voters to reflect arrogance, a lack of real knowledge, and a narrow view of the world. It took twenty years and Bill Clinton to overcome some of these opinions about the Democratic Party.

Even though Democrats were not successful nationally, politics continued to function on the local level. I made the acquaintance of Barbara and Rufus Phillips when I became active in the Virginia State Democratic Party. Through them and during Rufus' primary campaign for Congress, I met Martha and Matt Reese and later met Lynda and Chuck Robb. I also met Lucy Denney. Lucy and I would collaborate on campaigns through the 1970s, and we co-managed Congressman Joseph L. Fisher's last two campaigns for Congress. But we didn't begin on the same side.

Rufus asked me to manage his primary campaign for Congress. It was the first time I had complete responsibility for overseeing a campaign. We ran a respectable campaign, but the large Fairfax County base was split between Rufus and another member of the County Board of Supervisors. This split gave the majority of the solidly Democratic vote in Arlington County to Joseph L. Fisher, who won without a runoff. There was another candidate, from the fringes of society, who lent some humor to the race. He was a young radical and a political neophyte complete with earring and ponytail.

I was almost as green as this young man and still had not developed the acumen to determine if a candidate really did or did not have a good chance of winning. In some ways it seemed like a repeat for me of the frustrations I had felt over Boots's campaign. The numbers just did not add up. What I learned, mostly under Matt Reese's tutelage, was invaluable. It included basic campaign organization and focused on how to run a proper phone bank, track contributions, keep the books, handle a budget, and how not to talk to the press. My blunders were colossal. My first mistake was talking to the press. In order to get on the ballot in Virginia, a candidate had to submit a certain number of signatures from his or her district on petitions. The filing date, when petitions were delivered to the election board, came during a time when I had to be in Kansas City on Panel of American Women business, so I left my staff what I thought were specific instructions to get Rufus filed in a timely manner. But something happened, and our office was late in filing. This put Rufus' name at the bottom of the ballot, not a good place for it to be.

A young reporter who covered Northern Virginia for *The Washington Post* interrogated me about the filing. Not wanting to accuse my staff, I waffled but finally in frustration made what I thought was an off-the-cuff (and off-the-record) remark, "Gee, nobody's perfect." This was the only quote from me that was reported in the paper the next day. From then on, I made sure that the press talked only to the campaign's press secretary and not to me, the campaign manager. I would later amend my "no press" attitude when I was working on campaigns after the passing of the 1974 Federal Elections Campaign act. Since it was my job to file the

Federal Election Commission reports, I had the unenviable job of walking the press through each filing. I invariably got involved with some young reporter who had to be educated about the entire process. To make things worse, the reporters' attitude was always one of "Aha! We've caught you trying to cheat" when in fact they didn't understand what they were reading.

Twice in my career I made the mistake of ordering printed material or mailing lists over the phone. Both times resulted in disaster and cost us money we could have used elsewhere. In the case of Rufus' campaign, we finished $20,000 in the hole, and I spent the next year helping the Phillipses dig out of the debt. One of the best exercises for me was to call on all the vendors to whom we still owed money. The small vendors we paid first and in full. We had to pay some vendors (such as the C&P Telephone Company) in full because otherwise it would become classed as a corporate contribution. Others we paid an agreed-on percentage of what we owed.

Thus, I was raising money to pay off creditors and for Rufus' upcoming campaign for reelection to the Fairfax County Board of Supervisors. Like so many candidates who run for a lower office after reaching for a higher one, he had lost support. The afternoon of the Board election, we were at the Phillips' home, and I remarked to Conrad Marshall, one of Rufus' strongest supporters, that I would call someone and get them out to the vote if I only had the energy. Too bad I didn't at least call my husband and Rufus' secretary. You just never know who will vote and who will not get to the polls despite the best of intentions. When we tallied the votes being called in from the precincts, I could not believe it. We were eight votes behind—eight votes! I did not need the Bush/Gore race to teach me that every vote counts. The county tallies confirmed our own count. There was a state-mandated recount that resulted in no change despite protests to specific votes, including one absentee ballot cast just before one of our supporters died in the hospital. The recount was to no avail.

The following year, Joe Fisher's campaign approached me. John Milliken took me to lunch and asked me if I would co-chair the fundraising for Joe's re-election campaign in 1976. I was flattered beyond belief that the Congressman wanted my help since I had run the last campaign against him. Throughout that campaign I maintained cordial dealings with the staff of Joe's first race. His campaign manager and I became acquainted when the longhaired hippie who was a third candidate in this race accused Joe and Rufus of sending subliminal sexual messages in the images used in their literature. While I do not deny some campaigns or consultants might try something like that, it was completely foreign to our own candidates' personalities and inclinations. Joe's manager and I discussed the matter—and dismissed it—amid gales of laughter at the prospect of either dignified candidate being a sex object.

The 1976 Fisher race was a joy from beginning to end. Our headquarters were housed in a defunct massage parlor. Before setting up shop, we first had to get rid of the huge hot tub in the middle of the space and peel the mirrors off the ceiling. This was where I met Paddy McLaughlin, who was not only a talented artist but a great campaign manager. Among my cohorts were Lucy Denney and Jean McDonald (Joe's press aide) and a host of Arlington citizens who made the Democratic Party a powerhouse in Arlington. Lucy and I formed a great team, and we co-managed Joe's campaigns in 1978 and 1980; the first was successful, the second was a loss.

Since Virginia elects its state and local officers on the off year from federal elections, I was busy each year.

I helped in a number of races for county supervisor and began my association with Chuck Robb as his fundraiser for the primary of his Lieutenant Governor's race. Chuck and I became acquainted when we were Democratic-party precinct captains of neighboring precincts and rode to meetings together.

In his Lieutenant Governor's primary, four of us worked out of the Robbs' basement. They included Scooter Miller, an old friend of Lady Bird Johnson; Pat Mayer, the wife of Chuck's one-time commander in the Marine Corps; Caroline Reed; and me. Scooter helped with personal solicitations for campaign funds; she had a wealth of general information along with her organizing skills. Pat acted as Chuck's personal assistant, overseeing all of his correspondence. She would remain his personal assistant through his tenure as lieutenant governor, governor, and senator, retiring only after his defeat in 2000. Caroline acted as scheduler and dealt with the Secret Service when Mrs. Johnson was in town.

The real campaign office was in Richmond. After a rocky start, Chuck put together a wonderful team, some of whom, like Jane Vitray, remained with him all the way through his career or at least until the senatorial elections. There was an exceptional army of volunteers who made up most of the campaign staff; this was the original "Robb Mob." With only a few exceptions, these were the faces I saw on election night in 2000 when Chuck finally lost an election.

After Chuck won the 1977 primary, Sandy Duckworth took over from me as fundraising chair, and I did special events, including a dinner honoring then Vice President Mondale and his wife Joan, whom I had known through the Junior League and from working at the National Gallery. It was a beautiful dinner, held at the home of one of Chuck's supporters in Alexandria.

About this time, Lady Bird Johnson came up from Texas to help campaign for her son-in-law. Her Secret Service man, Jim Harden, accompanied her. We were standing in the campaign office in front of a printing press loaned to us by one of the unions. We never used the thing, and it took up a lot of room.

"Where did you get that?" Jim asked me.

I explained and asked "Why?"

"Because this is the kind of press we usually pick up when we arrest forgers."

I suggested perhaps he could pinch some plates and paper for us to print our own money since we had the press. It seemed a much easier way to raise money than asking for it. Incorruptible as always, Jim declined.

Matt Reese's friendship afforded me some rare and precious opportunities. First, he called me one day and said, "Janet, remember when you were going to have the president of the United States address the Jefferson/Jackson day dinner, and at the last moment you had to ask the county Democratic chair to make the speech?" Of course, this had never happened to either one of us, but I knew exactly what he was talking about, since I, too, had planned enough events with and for politicians who did not show. "Well," he said, "it's happened to me, and I want to know if you will make the main address at the American Association of Political Consultants banquet."

"About what?"

"Being a volunteer."

I made the speech, and three superb things happened. First, I received a standing ovation, much to my surprise. Second, I met many of the consultants who would become my good friends over the next few years. Finally, Jamie Auchincloss took a terrific picture of me wearing my boa and the dress printed with a design of turkey feathers. Not long after the dinner, Matt Reese nominated me to be a member of the Board of the American Association of Political Consultants. I loved serving with those consultants, Democrats and Republicans. It was also without doubt the most disorganized group of people I have ever been associated with, even including the Panel of American Women. It was my privilege to serve as its secretary for two terms and as secretary of the International Association for one term. The end of those terms is part of the story of the 1980s.

The best years were the ones when Roy Pfautch was president and I was secretary. We were two old campaign managers. We did manage to impose some order on the group and got them off dead center. We instituted a newsletter that I badly edited since I was a complete amateur, but I relied on the talent of Paddy McLaughlin, who had prepared Joe Fisher's printed materials. Roy conceived of the "Poly awards" and pushed until they were established. The Polys are given for outstanding campaign consulting in several fields, including television, radio, print outdoor advertising, direct mail, and several other categories. In those first years, the judges were usually Roy, me, and one other person, even though none of us were media people.

Bob Squier complained loudly that he was not going to submit anything for competition until the awards would be judged by a committee of his peers. Of course, he was right. We just didn't have either the time or the energy to come up with another modus operandi. Despite his complaints, Bob was a loyal board member. Once, after spending a seminar educating the AAPC on the vagaries of the 1974 Campaign Finance Act, he and I were walking down the hall together. He asked me, "So how do you like being a member of a regulated industry?" I laughed, and we agreed that as with all campaign laws, if you worked in the business, you learned to adjust to the changes.

"This one," he added more soberly, "will probably make us run campaigns the way we always should have done." I was pleased that Congress had put up some guardrails in addition to the Hatch Act and the prohibition of accepting foreign contributions. I could never have conceived that the Supreme Court would throw everything out in its Citizens United decision.

AAPC board meetings were always a hoot and took place in wonderful locations—a mansion on the Eastern Shore of Maryland, Las Vegas, or Marina del Rey. We were such a group of children, swapping war stories, and we even had a food fight at one dinner in Washington.

The last four years of the decade were the Carter years. When Carter was elected, Boots and I and our friends, the Salzmans and the Reeses, dressed in our finest attire and rode the Metro to downtown Washington to attend one of the inaugural balls. We had a great time, but I would never repeat it. Inaugural parades, on the other hand, were always worth seeing. As for the ceremony itself, I have arrived at the age when watching it on television at home seems much better than freezing in the January rain and snow.

Historians agree that Carter was not an outstanding president. I would not argue that he was an outstanding one, but I would argue that he was one of the most misunderstood of our presidents. His honesty and sincerity made him hard for America to take. They didn't know what to do with him whether they were liberals or conservatives. As soon as he was elected, I was surprised to see a Herblock cartoon in *The Washington Post* depicting the White House with an old rubber tire swing hanging from a tree. That wonderful cartoonist had caught not the truth but the false view of Carter.

Nixon's family entertained his bowling buddies in the White House, and the Fords carried on much of their genteel country-club existence there, but the Carters were people of great sophistication and culture. Amy and Rosalynn Carter attended the Kennedy Center regularly. Most US presidents and their families never attend a performance unless the occasion is the Presidential Awards or something like that. One evening I received a call from a friend who said that the Carters were not going to use their tickets to a performance, and would we like to go and sit in the presidential box? Naturally we went. I can report that it is a very comfortable box and has its own bathroom.

Boots and I went to the Carter White House a number of times, once for a lovely evening of classical music following a state dinner. We had not been invited to be guests at the dinner but were asked to attend the concert that followed. In the summer, when the Carters hosted groups of gospel singers on the White House lawn, we wandered around the grounds listening to the various choirs. Most of the attendees were white and affluent like us and had given generously to the Democratic party. From what was reported on the evening television news, a viewer would think the entire crowd had been African American. It gave the impression that the president was pandering to a constituency rather than thanking donors. Perhaps neither of those views was entirely acceptable to the public.

I met Rosalynn Carter a number of times and always found her gracious. The ugliest thing the mean members of the Republican Party could say about her was to use the "Iron Magnolia" epithet, which was something of a compliment to her, I thought. I was never aware that any of the ugly sexual smears that were so often leveled at other Democratic First Ladies from Eleanor Roosevelt to Hillary Clinton were being used against her. The Democrats were pikers in this arena. All they ever said about Nancy Reagan was that she was a clotheshorse, and they actually liked Barbara Bush and Betty Ford.

The first time I met Mrs. Carter was during the 1976 campaigns when she was scheduled to come to the Washington area for an appearance. She was to go first to Maryland. The Carter campaign called me at the Fisher headquarters in Falls Church from their Atlanta campaign office. They were drumming up bodies to appear at a rally, but I pointed out that they had Mrs. Carter scheduled to be in suburban Maryland on Yom Kippur. I didn't think it was appropriate, given the number of Jewish voters in the area. We finally settled on an appearance in Northern Virginia that I had to organize. She was to address a group of Hispanic voters there. We turned out a good crowd, and she spoke entirely in Spanish.

As for President Carter, his honesty about the energy crisis and America's "malaise," as the press put it, just didn't sell. Yet Americans are always loudly complaining that politicians won't talk straight to them—go figure. His generosity and commitment to the public good made him a beloved figure after his presidency.

While I remained engaged in political campaigns and Boots was engaged with his law practice, our children were becoming teenagers. Sarah was about to graduate from Madeira. The summer before her junior year, the boys were in camp in Vermont. On our way to pick them up we took Sarah on a college tour that included Vassar, Smith, Mount Holyoke, and Dartmouth. I had visions of my daughter going to a women's college; after all, that had been my dream. As luck would have it, we spent the first night with a Panel friend in New Haven. The next morning, my friend insisted on giving us a tour of Yale. For Sarah it was like falling in love; I could see it in her face. None of the other colleges we visited elicited any enthusiasm from her; she was determined to go to Yale.

She did, and in her second year she met Ed DeLeon. We first met him in November of 1978 when he arrived at our house carrying tails, white tie, and proper shoes to escort Sarah to the cotillion in Washington where she made her debut. What an introduction to the family that was. We all endured the test and went on to become better acquainted in circumstances that were not quite so pretentious.

Henry found his niche at Langley High School, first working as a "tech" in the drama department and then finding the courage to try out for parts. His senior year he was Judd in *Oklahoma*, and Craig Frawley, who already had an Equity card at eighteen, sang the role of Curly. It was an outstanding performance. Lynda Robb, Caroline Reed, and I went, and we cheered and cheered. Craig would later star in the road company of *Cabaret* with Joel Gray, but tragically he was one of the first of the many young artists and performers who succumbed to AIDS.

Will was still playing baseball. Our summers in Wisconsin were arranged around the All-Star Little League season. He was usually on the team, but 1976 was a sad exception. Will loved to dive and was swimming at the Washington Country Club when he fell off the ladder to the three-meter board and broke his leg. The accident occurred just before the All-Star games and during the middle of the Democratic Convention in New York City where Jimmy Carter was renominated. Fortunately, we had a young woman staying at the house along with Maxine. Between the two of them, they got him to the hospital and to a doctor who put the leg in a cast and contacted us. As consolation, Will had the opportunity to attend his first Democratic Convention. We hired a limousine because it was too hard to get him and his crutches in and out of a taxi; we picked him up at the airport, and took him to the convention. We had a wonderful time, but he was in a cast all summer.

Never one to sit idly, Will later broke the cast tramping through the woods in Wisconsin, and we had to trek down to Wausau to have another one put on. Eventually the leg mended. As a result, he could not run quite as fast as he could formerly, but he did learn to do needlepoint. I had been desperate to find something he could do while he stayed quiet.

Life was good to us then. On the surface, everything appeared to be perfect.

Chapter 16

ADDICTION AND RECOVERY

THE DARK SIDE to our happy family circle was that I continued to drink, and by the end of the 1970s my drinking was completely out of control. This was apparent to my family, but like many alcoholics I continued to be highly functional. Alcoholism has little to do with appearances. It is impossible to describe addiction to someone who has never experienced it. Unless you know first-hand the grinding, oppressive desire that drives you to a hit or to a drink, it is impossible to imagine. Once my niece's husband, a doctor, asked me about alcoholism. "Well," I said, "I can tell you, but it's like my telling you what it is like to be pregnant. If you haven't experienced it personally, you cannot know."

It all started innocently enough. Oklahoma was a dry state, but there was always alcohol in my parents' home. My father made wine in the basement. When he and my mother were first married, he also tried making beer. After all, he was a chemist by trade, so what could go wrong? It exploded all over the kitchen, and my mother was displeased in the extreme. He had better luck with the wine, but it was highly acidic and tasted like what I would come to know as a poor-grade Chianti. Still, it was loaded with alcohol, the only thing he cared about. They kept a decently stocked liquor cabinet, but to my knowledge, mother never took a drink or ever served alcohol unless the family had dinner guests. My father made regular trips to the basement where the stash was kept. His behavior did not seem out of the ordinary to me, but as I grew older, I became more aware of what he was doing. Once, after a long—and for my father, unusual—cocktail hour with his broker, he sat at the breakfast room table and had a crying jag. I don't even remember what the subject of his remorse or regret was, I only recall the incident; I must have been about fourteen.

By the age of sixteen, I had already experienced the wonderful gift that wine gave me when we were in Italy. Alcohol made me feel free. Whatever trouble I may have had seemed to melt in its glow. It was also, for me, a social lubricant. I hung out with the guys who drank and felt very grown up. I started to smoke at the same time but did not smoke or drink at home.

By the time I was in college, I began to smoke in front of my parents. My father, who hadn't smoked in thirty years, started again. He immediately lost about twenty-five pounds from his 170-pound frame and quit a second time for good. I could not see that smoking had much effect on me, so I enjoyed every puff. In college I continued to party, but as in high school, I maintained a high grade average and learned how to look responsible while I drank far more than was good for me. In college I experienced my first blackouts. This is a type of alcohol-induced amnesia that enabled me to walk, talk, drive a car, and do almost anything before I passed out. But the next day I would have no memory of what I had said or done.

For people who are recovering alcoholics, these episodes are the really scary memories—or the lack of them. We could have done anything during those blackouts and would never know or remember a thing, possibly including killing someone in an auto accident. Sexual acting out often happens in blackouts too, although I didn't seem to be inclined to pick up men when I was drinking. However, I did plenty of necking with my dates, drunk or sober.

Even though my mother was concerned about my drinking in college, she didn't say anything until after I graduated and got married. The fact that she did not mention it at the time is worth noting. She rarely said anything to my father about his drinking in front of the rest of us although I don't know what she said in private. As I became older, she would tell me how he had embarrassed her when they were out. My father, like all alcoholics, felt freer and better when he drank, and sometimes alcohol led him out of his usual quiet and contained state into garrulousness. She hated his behavior when he drank and thought he always bragged too much when he imbibed alcohol. I always thought he was just funny. He had a very wry sense of humor, and it came out when he had a little to drink.

After I married, I stopped drinking for a year, first because I was still recovering from mononucleosis and then simply because Boots was concerned about anyone's drinking too much. He had seen both of his uncles drink more often than was good for them. Also, he felt it was something of an occupational hazard for trial lawyers. At the time, he was mostly doing litigation. This was fine with me. I was busy and started having babies. We did go out frequently on weekends. I would drink, and he would eat.

Sometimes I drank more than I intended. Then, when we could afford a babysitter, we both began to sing in the All Souls Choir. Not only was it a "partying bunch," but we would stop off after choir practice at a little jazz club off May Avenue where a fine pianist had an outstanding combo. At other times we would go to another piano bar, and I would drink and sing, doing both badly.

We looked good on the surface, but I was lacerating the family. Boots and the children never knew what sort of mood I would be in. Would I be mellow? Would I be sarcastic? Would I be seething with rage? Usually, it was the latter.

I had hit emotional bottom about five years before I found the means to quit. Mr. Boots, my father-in-law, had contracted pneumonia, and he suddenly became senile. He was living with us, and he did not know where he was. He would get up in the middle of the night and begin to dress. By this time, he didn't even know us, but we attempted to take care of him at home. His bout of pneumonia happened in the middle of the winter. That spring, Sarah went to France to study for part of the semester in a program sponsored by the Madeira School.

At the same time, Boots was scheduled to go to South Africa on business. He naturally had the major burden of seeing to his father's physical care. His absence would leave Maxine, who did not drive a car; the boys; and me at home with Mr. Boots. Maxine was incapable of handling him. He had to be bathed, and he had to be helped in the bathroom.

I did not think I could cope with the situation, so before Boots left I took him to dinner and pleaded with him to find a proper nursing home. He promised to do so, but somehow time passed, and he left on his trip. While Boots was gone, I found a place where my father-in-law could live; it was not that good, but it was acceptable. In those days there were few nursing homes, and most of them were horrible. So when Boots returned from South Africa I demanded we put his father in the nursing home. Sarah returned from Europe, and one evening I got very drunk and created an awful scene. My fury at having been left in that situation came out in a terrible burst of anger. All three children were brought into the fight; it was a night to remember.

The next morning, to his credit Boots said he would do anything he could to help me. I asked him to walk down the block and talk to one of the three psychiatrists who lived in our neighborhood.

The result was a referral to a psychiatrist in Washington with whom I met for more than two years. We did a lot of good work, and every time I would suggest I had done enough work he would say, "And how is your drinking?"

Naturally I would say, "Just fine."

Actually, on two occasions between the time I hit bottom and when I finally stopped drinking, I had managed to put together ten months without having a drink. I was dry, but not sober. The second time I slipped back into drinking came about when my sister-in-law Marilyn and I went to Europe. We spent a week in London and a week in Paris. Just before we left France, we went out for a really fine dinner. Since she did not drink and needed to eat early because of her hypoglycemia, we had eaten our evening meal in brassieres, and I had not been tempted to drink. But that evening in a good Parisian restaurant, I ordered wine.

The next day, during a visit to the Sacre Coeur church, my passport case was stolen or lost—I don't really know which. And tucked inside my passport case was my airline ticket. I was in an extreme state of agitation. We went first to the prefecture of police and gave a hilarious account in very broken French to a most attractive policeman who looked like Burt Reynolds. He took all our information, and then someone burst into his office, rattling away rapidly in French. Our officer stood up, put a pistol in his belt, and ran out of the office, saying something about chasing "the criminals."

That had nothing to do with us, but we had the paperwork from the police, so we went to the American Embassy. It was Sunday, but luckily they had staff for such emergencies. They sent me to a place where I could get a photo taken for a few francs. It reminded me of the booths at the fair where we used to put a quarter in and get our pictures taken. With the photograph and Marilyn's signed affidavit that affirmed I was who I said I was, I received a temporary passport. The next day I talked my way onto the plane. That passport picture was truly frightening; I must have looked like a mad woman. I still look at it every once in a while to remind myself what I looked like at the most frazzled end stage of my drinking. The wine and the tension I felt put me right back where I had been earlier with my drinking.

Most people associate drinking alcohol with happy times such as family occasions, happy hours, or a companionable drink with a friend after work. It is easy to forget that alcohol is a depressant. For the drinker, the period of well-being or euphoria lasts a shorter and shorter time, and more alcohol is needed to achieve the goal. When the good feelings pass the alcoholic is left in a state of depression.

By the summer of 1979 I had begun to experience periodically the cruel pain of real depression. One summer evening at the lake, I was upstairs with a glass of scotch and soda. I could hear the children downstairs laughing at something on television. I reached the point where I believed they would be better off without me. I just wanted the world to stop and let me off—anything to get beyond the mental and spiritual pain I was in.

I went to the closet and took down Boots's handgun. I fingered the leather holster but didn't unsnap it. The prospect of the mess was too much for me. As it happened, that summer Boots had a series of particularly severe ear infections, and I knew there were two partial bottles of opioids in the medicine cabinet. I took all of them with the scotch. I expected to fall into a peaceful and permanent sleep. The opposite happened; I became wired. The pills threw me into a nearly manic state of hyper awareness. All I could do was lie in bed listening to my heartbeat and breath. I finally did fall asleep, exhausted.

That experience had a profound effect on what I did three months later. I had reached the point every alcoholic comes to if they truly want to get sober. I had faced the question "do I want to live or die?" Finally, in November of 1979, things came to a head. My relationship with Boots had become more and more strained. Generally, we got along well and did not argue much until I took a drink. Then it was awful. We went to marriage counseling, and the counselor asked me if I had tried AA. I said, no, but perhaps I would be willing to try. I said I just did not want AA to "change my life." I would eventually discover what a stupid remark that was.

One Saturday evening Boots and I went to dinner and got into the usual argument. I always refer to it as "the fight." I don't recall what it was really about; it just seemed to be the same fight we always had, with no resolution. Usually, I was in a blackout by that time and would remember nothing the following day of what had been said.

This evening, he was just a little more inebriated than I was. He said, "You are the problem. You have the flaw." I knew what he was talking about. "I'll show him," I thought, "I'll stop drinking." But, the very next evening, I poured myself a glass of wine. I clearly remember staring at it. It was white wine in a balloon glass. I drank only half of it; it was the only drink I remember leaving half finished. The thought came very clearly to me: "This has got to stop."

The next day I phoned a friend who had stopped drinking. I asked her if she was going to AA, and she said she was.

"I would like to go with you sometime," I said. "I'll pick you up at seven o'clock," she replied. I went to my first meeting on November 19, 1979. My friend gave me the "Big Book," published in 1939 by the founder of AA and its first members. The book has had several revisions, but it remains the primary textbook for recovery from alcohol addiction and is the basis for other twelve-step programs.

After the meeting I went home, sat on the couch in the family room, and read the entire book. For the first time in my life, I understood what was wrong with me. The next day I promised my friend I would attend a meeting at my church, St. Dunstan's. That morning, I had an appointment with a printer. I was working on a local campaign and went with the campaign manager to interview someone we had not worked with before. I felt shaky and nervous; I hadn't expected to have withdrawal symptoms.

While we were sitting in the office of the man with whom we had the appointment, his phone rang. He answered it, and a quiet, rather cryptic conversation ensued. When he hung up, he apologized, saying that he did some counseling and always took such calls. "What kind of counseling?" I blurted. "Alcohol and drug counseling," he replied. "I went to my first AA meeting last night," I said, completely ignoring the campaign manager. She just sat there, a stunned observer of our conversation.

He listened to me and gently answered a number of questions I had about the disease of alcoholism and about AA. Then we finished our printing business. As I left the building and walked to my car, I looked up. It was one of those perfectly pristine fall days; the sky was a vivid blue. Suddenly I knew that the encounter was no accident. It was, I believed, an act of God, one of those many coincidences, synchronicities, or miracles of life that happen to all of us if we are aware enough to observe them.

Somehow, I knew my life had profoundly changed, and it gave me the strength to walk into that Tuesday-night meeting by myself. The decade of the 1970s ended on my forty-second day of sobriety. I chose a twelve- step recovery program. I did indeed stop drinking, but I also found a new way to live. I often describe it as spiritual yoga; you have to practice it to see results. My life became much more manageable and serene, but it wasn't easy; it took work.

Chapter 17

ANOTHER SHARP TURN

ON CHRISTMAS OF 1979 we took the children and went to Oklahoma for a visit with old friends and the few family members who remained in the city. We had a good time, but neither Boots nor I had any idea of returning there to live. He had recently left Casey, Lane, & Mittendorf, which was going through its own reorganization. He made a connection with a Boston-based firm, but he was not pleased with the arrangement. In Oklahoma City, I went to AA meetings where I found some old friends and former drinking buddies. I felt very much at home in the program there.

In February, Bob Hefner, president of Glover-Hefner-Kennedy Exploration, which everyone called GHK, asked Boots to come to Oklahoma City to serve as general counsel to the company. Most of Boots's practice in Washington had to do with oil and gas. He and Matt Reese and a friend, Bill Bracket, had worked hard on an Arctic gas project and on the decades-old suit that involved El Paso Natural Gas.

During the late 1970s, Bob spent many weeks at our house in McLean, using Boots's office as a base and lobbying for the deregulation of natural gas. Although there were others interested in the effort, Bob spearheaded it and got it all done.

We considered the offer, and Boots asked me how I would feel about moving back to Oklahoma City. I thought about all the possibilities and concluded that it felt like something I should do. My brother Thurman had spent all those years after my father's death managing the MT Myers Trust. Somehow, I thought it was time for me to know what was behind the money coming in every month.

Just the year before, Thurman and I had discussed the danger of having only one set of files to contain the data on all our mineral properties. The great oil boom of the late 1970s was just beginning. His oldest daughter, Valerie, went to work for her father and duplicated every scrap of paper—all of the mineral deeds, division orders, corporation commission orders, and correspondence. Thurman made a trip to Washington to help me get them in order by making file folders and explained to me what I was looking at. He created a system for managing our oil and gas interests that worked well.

His visit was pleasant. In earlier years, his drinking had been so bad and his behavior so unpredictable that I told him I didn't want him in my house. Now, however, he had nearly stopped drinking and was deeply into new-age matters and meditation. Tragically, he would die at sixty-nine from a cancer related to his drinking. But at this time his personality had taken a dramatic turn for the better. With his help, I began to take care of my own leasing and to make a few business decisions.

We had always kept our accounting in Oklahoma City, since we had to pay taxes in the state during the years we lived away. I needed a dependable accountant, a lawyer, and a banker in Oklahoma City. Later I would add a broker-manager for the commercial property, along with a building manager and an assistant for him. I didn't realize it at the time, but I was about to go into business.

It took me a year to complete our move from Washington, DC, to Oklahoma City. Boots moved in March of 1980 while I continued to work in Joe Fisher's reelection campaign and flew to Oklahoma about once a month. In July we bought a house on Hillcrest Avenue across the street from his parents' former house. Ours was a strange-looking house that had been built onto extensively. We set about renovating it, putting in a pool and building a tornado shelter. I didn't want to move back to the prairies without somewhere to hide.

Henry was at the University of Oklahoma, so he saw his father on weekends. The summer of 1980 he went to work in the oil fields at one of GHK's pipe yards in Elk City. One weekend tornadoes chased him all the way to Oklahoma City, so he and Boots left the little apartment Boots was renting and took shelter in the newly completed "hidey-hole," where they found our house painter with all of his family already ensconced.

By the summer of 1981 the Oklahoma City house was completed, and Will graduated from Langley High School in Virginia. My job with Joe Fisher's campaign ended in November 1980 with Joe's defeat. I was sorry to lose the campaign. His and Rufus' had been my only defeats, and when Joe lost, I felt that the nation had lost one of its truly great public servants. Reagan's election made it a bad year for Democratic moderates. The baby boomers voted in great numbers, and they were always negative voters. They were almost impossible to educate; this generation that had grown up during the Vietnam War had political sensitivities that had the density of concrete.

Carter lost the 10th District of Virginia to Reagan by 30,000 votes, and Joe lost by only 3,000 to Frank Wolf. But those votes were mostly in the new Stirling Park area that was inhabited by young families who had just moved to Virginia or to the DC area. We tried to do everything possible to win and bombarded the area with canvassing and targeted mail. I kept a log of the mailings used in the campaign. The headquarters put out a total of 450,000 pieces of mail during the election season.

In November I got my one-year AA chip, a bronze medallion bearing the Roman numeral I on one side. I continued to go to AA meetings, although I didn't do much about "working the steps." The previous spring, Boots and I had joined Joellen and Dan Hagge, friends from Wisconsin, on the *Queen of Sheba* to sail in the Caribbean. We were joined by friends from San Antonio and a couple from Missouri. I had known the Texas couple from SMU and had even been involved in their wedding. We had not seen each other for twenty-five years. We had a wonderful time, but what a difference there was from the last time I had seen my old friends. I had been horribly drunk on champagne at their wedding reception and had thrown up all over the house of the patient people with whom I stayed. The sailing trip went by without anyone commenting that I wasn't downing the wine everyone else was drinking. I realized most people don't care at all what you have to drink, so long as they get what they want.

There were exceptions. Earlier, in February 1980, Boots and I were invited to a house party at Wintergreen, a resort community on the Virginia Skyline Drive. The couple who owned the condo there was originally from Texas, and Boots had met the husband through his oil and gas work. They arranged for us to ride down to Wintergreen with a couple whom we didn't know. It was a delightful trip.

This couple drove us down to the house party in their limousine. They were originally from California and often took their several children from Washington to California by car. Instead of buying the usual station wagon they bought the limousine, so when the kids were noisy, they just rolled up the window between the passenger unit and the front seat. They let the children work out their problems.

I thought the husband looked familiar, but I just couldn't place him. I always made it a habit to try to forget where I met people since those who attend twelve-step meetings prefer to remain anonymous. Someone's drinking habits should be their own private business. When we arrived at the condo, our host was making Bloody Marys from his special mix that had the consistency of a gazpacho. I asked for mine without alcohol. He insisted on keeping the alcohol. I resisted, and finally he handed me a glass and walked off.

I gingerly put it to my nose and prepared to take a sip, still suspicious. But the kind gentleman who had driven us down was sitting at the bar next to me, and I heard his quiet voice say, "Pour it out." I looked at him, poured the drink down the sink, and made my own "Virgin Mary." We never said another word to each other about it, but I saw our driver occasionally at a meeting I would attend in McLean.

I continued my road to recovery through the back-and-forth year of relocating. The job of packing the house in Virginia with its fifteen years of accumulation was left to me. By then we had moved enough to be as used to moving as anyone could be. I was reminded of a remark Lee Udall made to me shortly before she and Stuart moved to Arizona. He and one of the boys packed their station wagon and literally put a mattress on its top. She protested, and Stuart said, "That's the way the Okies traveled." Her response was, "The only people I know from Oklahoma move with United Van Lines." By June the house had been sold. We moved and then went to Wisconsin for a short vacation.

Chapter 18

SETTLING IN

ONCE WE WERE established in Oklahoma City, I opened an office, and for the first year my niece Adrian worked for me and helped me get settled. The next year her sister Valerie came to work for me and brought some much-needed organization to my operation. She worked for me until her son Stuart was born, and then she and her husband Neil and Stuart all moved to New Jersey so Neil could finish his training at Columbia Presbyterian Hospital.

Her move brought two important things into my life. First, I hired Jennie Wynne as my assistant and secretary. Then Valerie left her fourteen-year-old cat Samantha with me. Sam lived to be about twenty-seven, and Jennie was still my right-hand person after more than twenty-five years. I hired her mostly because she knew a lot more about the oil business than I did. At the time, her husband Bill said to her, "You? Work for a woman? That'll last six months." That was in 1983. We reminded him of his remark yearly until his death in 2000.

The trust I took over consisted of the original mineral deeds I had typed after leaving college; the additional minerals that had been left for Thurman and me by both our parents; and the two Norman, Oklahoma, buildings on Campus Corner. The corner building was the first one my father had built after he had obtained the land with the old farmhouse on it. The second building next door was relatively new. My father rented it to a local firm that had several locations. The firm handled all sorts of supplies and was like an early Walmart; one of its supplies was paint. That first building burned to the ground in the 1960s. One evening around nine Thurman called me and said, "Turn on the television. Isn't that our building?" The four of us jumped in a car and sped to Norman.

We were not concerned about the corner building because our father had built it of solid masonry. In fact, it escaped the fire with no damage at all. The only thing Thurman, Marilyn, Boots, and I could do after we raced to the scene was to watch the fire until the building was reduced to twisted metal beams. Thurman saw to getting its replacement built and rented. The concrete construction of the corner building had saved it from the fire, but it was difficult to renovate and therefore difficult to rent.

"Why don't you renovate the second floor and make it into offices?" Boots suggested after I started to manage the properties. "Perhaps some of the faculty would like to have an office off campus." I liked the suggestion and spent a year renovating the building. Faculty members were not interested, but I did find a number of small businesses that were happy to have space close to campus.

In 1984 the price of oil tanked. By 1985 the boom of the 1970s had disappeared like melting snow. Businesses closed, especially the wonderful specialty shops that had sprung up along with the affluence of the boom. In order not to have to borrow money, I went back to the habits I formed after

I got married. I made a budget for the business, and each week I posted every expense it incurred. There were times I wondered if I could pay office rent and meet Jennie's payroll. I lived on what was left over and even moved my office to Norman in an unoccupied suite in the corner buildings to avoid paying rent.

At the time the highway on which I had to commute was under construction, and the trip was brutal. When I could afford it, Jennie and I moved the office back to Oklahoma City. By the end of the 1980s, I was debt free. About this time, I purchased a small shopping center in Norman. I got it by assuming the outstanding debt and paying about $20,000 in cash. The young couple that had built the center was forced to declare bankruptcy. My father had often said he was sorry he had not bought more property in Norman. I remembered what he said and took the plunge.

In addition to running the trust, I tried to keep up my political consulting. When Boots and I decided to move, he said he regretted that I had to leave my base in Washington. What I had started as a volunteer activity had progressed to my being paid for my work as a manager (which qualified me as a "political consultant"), and the next step was simply to be paid for my advice. But I thought I could consult from anywhere.

Actually, I did that for a while. I consulted on the campaign of a young woman who was running for governor and worked on the original "Liquor by the Drink" campaign. I made friends in the political community on whom I would need to call in the future. A "Liquor by the Drink" campaign might seem an unusual choice for someone in recovery, but as I indicated earlier, Oklahoma's liquor laws were complicated. Alcohol use in Oklahoma was regulated in such a way that enforcing it was more than problematic. For instance, you could not purchase a single drink in a restaurant. We still had some dry counties. Some of us felt these laws actually added to the hazards of drinking and driving. The proposal was state-wide. Its original version did not get onto the ballot, and I strongly disagreed with the version that finally passed. It was a proposal with "county option," which meant people could still drive to a county that was not "dry" and drive home tanked up with alcohol.

I disliked working as a consultant in Oklahoma. The voter-registration system was a mess, and the election boards seemed to be back in the stone age. There were none of the computerized tools I was used to, and the Democrats were not in the least interested in putting any in place. It finally took the State of Oklahoma to straighten things out on the state level. In Virginia we worked from clean computer lists of registered voters. These files were generated by the state's elections board and were made available to all parties and candidates. Each party took the raw data of names and addresses and added telephone numbers and any other data the party had concerning the voters' political preferences. Each campaign paid the state a nominal sum for the service.

I thought it a great idea if Oklahoma would do the same thing. My first obstacle was the state party. They were aghast at the thought that we might charge a campaign for anything. Next, several of us called on the Oklahoma Board of Elections. The director heard us out and said that the Board was working on it. When I mentioned Virginia, he said, "Oh well, Virginia is the gold standard." "Good," I thought, "Maybe you should do it the same way."

My final consulting job was for a Supreme Court candidate in Nevada in the late 1980s. Matt Reese called and asked me if I would come and consult on fundraising. I received $1,000 a day plus expenses. This was the crowning accomplishment of my consulting career, and it was gratifying; the candidate won. In the meantime, Pam Fleischaker, whom

I had met in the Muskie campaign, called me. She and David moved to Oklahoma City the year before we did. David had grown up in Oklahoma City and returned to help with his family's business just as I had. Pam told me, "Get down to Planned Parenthood. They need your help with fundraising." Partly because of her urgency and partly because I had nothing else to do and wanted to reconnect with a city where I had been deeply involved, I went.

I came to admire deeply the dedicated people who worked with Planned Parenthood. It is an unfortunate necessity that the fight to keep abortion a legal and safe option for women has obscured the ninety-eight percent of the organization's other wonderful works. Their primary mandate is maternal health. They serve the working poor, many of whom have no medical insurance. The typical patient used to be a married mother with one or two children. The demographics may have changed some, but I doubt that much is different today, except that there are now more single mothers. It is worth noting that the standing profile of a working mother is currently the profile of the vast majority of abortion patients. The enormous amount of preventative medicine Planned Parenthood provides saves its patients from agony, disability, and even death, and saves huge amounts of public money.

I thought it was wonderful to be able to help. The first person I met at Planned Parenthood of Central Oklahoma (PPCO) was Debbie Redwine, its dynamic young development director. She was trained as a sex educator and knew nothing about the mechanics of fundraising. She moved out of the development section because they desperately needed staff. Although she was unhappy about having to step into the job of providing education, to her great credit she was an apt student. Debbie became one of the best development directors I have known. In the end, she far surpassed her mentor, and her teaching skills made her an excellent trainer. Debbie and I had lots of fun doing workshops for Planned Parenthood. We developed a training course for Planned Parenthood's affiliates to train their boards how to ask for donations. We demonstrated the material at two regional conferences.

Despite insisting to everyone I would do training but would not go on the Board of Directors, I did just that. I subsequently became development chair and finally president of the affiliate. At each step I protested that I would not take the job. After my election as president, I settled down to do whatever the organization asked of me.

The first national workshop I attended was devoted to president's training. There I met Amy Cohen Denish, who was development director for the southern region. Amy was a dynamo. She recruited me to start mobilizing a group of volunteers to do fundraising training throughout the region. The Northeast Region had pioneered such a program. We set up our own program and printed brochures to be mailed to all the affiliates.

In truth, I did most of the training—and loved it. I traveled all over the South and Texas. In one of those incidents that you always remember, on the day the Challenger spacecraft blew up I stood in the office of Planned Parenthood's Nashville affiliate waiting for their development director and watched the tragic launch on the TV in their waiting room.

Eventually I also chaired the Southern Regional Nominating Committee. I made a couple of unsuccessful runs for the National Board of Directors, but there were just too many white women involved, and the Southern Region was dedicated to diversity. We were always wryly amused at how much the other regions talked diversity, but we were the only region that actually came close to those guidelines on our boards. Nationally, African Americans, Native Americans, WASPs, Jews, Latinas, and Asians were involved. It reminded me of my old Panel of American Women days, and the participants were just as open with each other.

In 1988 I attended a Planned Parenthood convention in St. Louis. I happened to notice the name tag of a young woman sitting behind me, Ngina Lythcott. The last name was familiar to me; it was the surname of the internationally known public-health physician Dr Lythcott who had taught at the University of Oklahoma Medical School. I knew that in the intervening years, he had lived in New York City. Earlier, he and his family had lived in Africa, where he had done amazing work in public health. I asked Ms. Lythcott if she was related, and she replied that he was her father. She also told me her first name had been Ruth when she lived in Oklahoma City, but in Africa she took the name Ngina.

She went on to say that her years growing up in Oklahoma City as a Black child had been the bitterest of her life. Her father had to drive her to an orthodontist in Tulsa, a hundred miles away, to find a dentist who would treat Black patients. Worst of all, she was an excellent student but was denied admission to Casady School, an elite private Episcopal school. "I have been asked to come to Oklahoma City to do a workshop," she said. "But I just don't think I can go back."

Then the two of us began to play, "who do you know?" She wanted to know where the Atkinses were? I told her Dr. Atkins was dean but that his wife Hannah was now the Secretary of State of the State of Oklahoma. I asked her if she had known Martina Cox; she had, and she inquired after Martina's son. I replied that he was in the Legislature. And Shirley Darrell and Lew? I told her that Lew had died, but Shirley had been elected County Commissioner. I added, "If you do come to Oklahoma City, you wouldn't find much has changed." Suddenly Ngina stopped and took me by the arm. "Listen to yourself," she said. "Listen to what you're saying! Things *have* changed." Then we both burst into tears.

Ngina ultimately agreed to do the workshop in Oklahoma City, and I had some people come in to visit. We had a great time. It was the last time I was the only white person in the room. The thing that always impresses me when I am the minority person in the Black community is the laughter.

I had one more opportunity to make a statement about civil rights. The Junior League had been an important part of my Washington stay. But the League in Oklahoma City seemed to me to have little sense of direction compared to the dynamic course of the Washington League. Perhaps I had simply lost interest. The last thing I did with the League was to help sponsor the acceptance of the first Black woman into the Oklahoma City group.

At the time, Anita Bridges was an attorney with Kerr-McGee, a graduate of Howard University and George Washington University Law, and she had preceded me as president of Planned Parenthood. In my opinion, she was a perfect candidate for the League. Under the rules as they were at that time, if a candidate obtained a sufficient number of sponsors, she was automatically admitted. I was at a Planned Parenthood meeting when Anita's acceptance was announced. Her sponsors had a luncheon for her, and they called me at the hotel to inform me. Anita was delighted, and I burst into tears. I think she was astonished at my reaction. It would have been impossible to explain how those of us felt who had tried so hard in the 1960s to bring a measure of fairness to the people and institutions of the United States. By the 1970s, there was a mutual feeling that although many laws had been passed, not the least of which was the Voting Rights Act, we had failed in many of our efforts.

I couldn't appreciate that such change is so slow, but change does occur. There is a long way to go for women like Ngina Lythcott and Anita Bridges, but the pace is continual. One look at the cabinets of Bill Clinton, George W. Bush, and Barack Obama proves the point. If the cabinet at this writing does not reflect the effort, the leadership of the opposition does.

Soon after we moved back to Oklahoma, Boots got a call asking him to serve on the Advisory Board of KCSC, the "good music" station sponsored by what was then Central State University in Edmond, Oklahoma, and is now called the University of Central Oklahoma. Boots declined and kindly suggested they ask me since I was the musician in the family. I had loved classical music since mother took me to opera and concerts, and I had always sung in church choirs. Thus began my long and satisfying association with a remarkable little radio station. I watched it grow from its stumbling on-air beginning—one student announcer had introduced Mozart's "Te Deum" as "Mozart's Tedium"—into what I still consider one of the best all-music classical stations in the country. Its growth and maturity, its expansion of its listening audience across much of the state, its production of segments that are now marketed nationally, its broadcasts on satellite radio, and its professionalism are all the work of Brad Ferguson, its station manager. Working with the station was a delight during my years in Oklahoma. I was glad to serve on its Advisory Board, but the benefits far outweighed the effort. For me, tuning in to the station was a sure path to sanity.

I also continued off and on to sing in church choirs, both at All Soul's and at St. Paul's Cathedral. Most consistently, I sang in the Canterbury Choral Society. This choral society was founded just after Boots and I had left for Washington, so it was well established by the time we moved back. Some 150 singers gave two concerts a year, and later we became the official chorus for the Oklahoma Symphony, enabling us to perform works as large as a Mahler symphony and to sing with world-famous artists. My dear friend Aileen Frank also got me involved with the outfit known as Chamber Music in Oklahoma. This group presented visiting chamber ensembles from all over the United States and sponsored six or seven concerts a year.

Aileen and I served on the board of KCSC at the same time. As we were sitting around before one meeting, she said, "I would like to go to Alaska." "So would I," I said. Dr. Les Arneson was at the table and settled all this by saying, "OK, let's go." Then in her eighties, Aileen was not able to walk far. Nevertheless, Les and Joanne Arneson, Aileen, and I took a Holland America cruise to Alaska. We did just fine with Aileen in a wheelchair part of the time. I was delighted to be whisked to the front of the line at the gate. While I walked or saw the sights, she sat contentedly on a park bench and watched the eagles.

I continued my support of the symphony orchestra and served twice on the Board of the Oklahoma City Philharmonic through two interesting times. The old Oklahoma Symphony Orchestra had been an institution I had known throughout my life. Mother and I went to its every concert from the time I was about eight years old. She was active with the Women's Committee of the Symphony, which supported the orchestra with its activities and fundraising. She had also served on its Board of Directors before she became too ill to attend meetings.

In the early 1980s, what had been the great oil boom became the great oil bust. Every institution in the state struggled for money. During the flush years, the Symphony provided full-time employment for its instrument-playing members, although many of them continued to teach privately to supplement their incomes. A militant group in the Musicians Union insisted on calling for more money and benefits for its members as the economy worsened. As a result, in about 1986 the Board of Directors voted to close up shop. They voted for "no orchestra" over "no money" and refused to bankrupt the organization. The assets that remained were given to the Orchestra League, which had begun as the Women's Committee.

Many of the young musicians were forced to find jobs in other communities. The older musicians found themselves subsisting on much-reduced incomes from teaching and whatever gigs they could find. One such gig was summer employment in the pit orchestra of Oklahoma City University's Lyric Theater musical productions. The associate conductor of the Symphony conducted those performances. Some of the older, more experienced union members begged him to see what he could do about getting another orchestra started. People needed jobs.

Joel called Jane Harlow, who had been a member of the old Oklahoma Symphony Orchestra's Board, and she in turn called a meeting of people who were interested in music. We met at the Petroleum Club, and she asked if we would help form a board for a new symphony orchestra. She explained that she could not be involved because there was an agreement between the Musicians Union and those interested in reforming an orchestra to the effect that no one who had served on the old OSO Board of Directors could serve on the new board for at least five years. Also, no one who had served on the union's strike committee would be hired for the new orchestra.

This arrangement was agreeable to all—except for the New York office of the Musicians Union. The old orchestra had provided full-time employment, and the new one would provide only half-time employment. The New Yorkers were afraid other orchestra boards around the country would take our arrangement as a precedent. The truth was that we didn't have enough money to pay full-time salaries, and the musicians were wondering how they would pay rent and buy food.

Thus began a fascinating two-year legal battle. Serving on our board was a lawyer named Charles Ellis. He was amiable and laconic and could put on a great "aw shucks" act. He was also a brilliant attorney. Charles' demeanor lulled the New York and the Austin lawyers for the union into assuming that the case would be easy for them to win. It wasn't. And to be sure, we had the support not only of our own board but of all the local musicians and the new union leadership. It took two years, but we finally got an orchestra. During this time, we hired Alan Valentine as manager, and he put together a superb staff. Naturally, I took on the job of training the board to ask for money, which we desperately needed. There were some very wealthy and important people who sat on the board, including such citizens as Bill Pirtle, CEO of Oklahoma Natural Gas. They were all troopers. They set to work, raised the money, and we were ready for business as soon as we got the word to go ahead from the legal department. It was a joy to serve on the orchestra's board, and I loved watching the orchestra grow both musically and as an organization. I resigned shortly before my term ended, because by then I was running the family business and going to school nearly full time.

Chapter 19

ONE LAST TRIP AROUND THE BLOCK

BOOTS'S LIFE WAS also changing. In 1984 his job with the gas-exploration company ended. The economic devastation in the oil business nearly took the company under, and its CEO Robert Hefner salvaged just enough for himself and one other executive. Everyone else, including Boots, was left only with severance pay and whatever remained of the working interests in the company they had bought into along with other employees.

Boots and I blew his severance pay on a trip around the world. Chuck Robb was governor of Virginia. He and his wife Lynda asked Boots to attend a trade conference with them in Japan. About a month later, the International Association of Political Consultants was scheduled to meet in Israel. We decided to go to Japan and just keep on going around the globe to Israel and then back home aboard the Concorde. I must say it was a wonderful trip.

Boots and I took the bullet train from Tokyo to Kyoto and back with all of our luggage—six weeks of clothes for a variety of climates. The Japanese travel with only a tote bag or one suitcase at most. However, there were porters available, and one of them loaded up all six of our cases on his head, arms, and back. All the way to the platform he groaned loudly, "AH. OH. AH. OH." But he got us on the train. The Kyoto hotel staff helped us with our luggage.

Kyoto is a marvelous and historic city. The conference was interesting; future president George H. W. Bush gave a memorable lecture on the need for free trade. Lynda Robb made it possible for the wives in the group to see some of the gardens that were usually closed to tourists. When we arrived back in Tokyo, the first person we saw was our porter. He looked at us and without picking up a bag groaned "AH. OH." But I suppose the tip we gave him when we left had been sufficient, because although he groaned, he took us, along with our luggage, all the way to the taxi.

From Tokyo we flew to Hong Kong. I had quit smoking, but the tension of the trip was getting to me. I bummed a cigarette from poor Boots, who knew what would happen. He had only brought along enough American cigarettes for himself. One would never be enough for me, and so between us we had only half of what we needed for the trip. I knew, though, that for me it was either a cigarette or a drink, and I did not want to toss away almost five years of sobriety. I smoked the cigarette and found an AA meeting in Hong Kong.

From Hong Kong we went to Bangkok, which I loved, and to Delhi, which I hated. The Thai are friendly, their country is beautiful, and they are clever craftspeople. I was knitting a sweater on the airplane, and while we waited to go through customs, I attracted a crowd of Thai women who wanted to watch what kind of stitches I was making. Thai silks, jewelry, and brass work are lovely. It was a surprise to find that the colorful decorations on their *stupas*, or temples, were made of pieces of broken pottery.

In India, the Sikhs were stirring up trouble. They never really threatened us, but they would walk around clanging their swords. Actually, our driver was a Sikh, and I felt safe with him. He was courteous, punctual, and always armed with the traditional *kirpan* as a weapon. What I really disliked about India was how the people treated each other. Any man vested with the least amount of authority—such as selling train tickets—seemed to assume the right to verbally abuse anyone trying to transact business. There was enormous contempt in the country for people of lower status, for foreigners, and for themselves. In any official capacity they seemed to be irritable, but they were quite friendly and accommodating as individuals.

Beggars, invalids, and lepers were everywhere. The traffic and pollution were horrible, and traveling from city to city in an automobile was one long game of "chicken." The roads were deplorable; they had no shoulders, and everyone tried to drive down the middle of the road, dodging oncoming traffic just in time, usually, to avoid a collision. The country did have its beauty. The saris were exquisite and made graceful flowers of the women who wore them. The pink city of Jaipur and the Taj Mahal were even more beautiful than one could imagine from any photograph.

From Delhi, we flew to Cairo via Kuwait City on Kuwait Airlines. At the time it was a superb airline that offered the best service I had experienced outside of Air China and the best food anywhere. Of course, since it was a Muslim country, there was no alcohol, which did not bother me. I was grateful for the extra emphasis on the cuisine.

I had warned Boots that Cairo would be dirty, crowded, and noisy, remembering what it was like when Shirley Salzman and I had taken a trip down the Nile three years earlier. But we arrived on a Saturday, the country's holy day, and there was no traffic. There were also few people on the street; after Delhi, it looked positively pristine. We had a beautiful trip down the Nile, and although we did not see some of the places

I had visited on my previous trip—Asyut, Beni Hassan, and Tel El Amarna—we saw plenty. Our tour group on the ship was small, and about eight of us sat together and mingled. One of the couples was from New York City. The husband was Jewish and loved bantering with the Arab children. He always bought strings of beads from the little Egyptian boys at each stop. Then, at the next stop he would give them away to the children and start the routine all over again by replenishing his stock of beads. At the last stop he overheard the men laughing about what a ridiculous thing that was. He sat quietly beside me and asked in a low voice, "Who am I to teach others how to be charitable?" Suddenly his lovely plan to help the children became clear. Later I would write this up in a short story.

From Cairo we went on to Israel. As members of the International Association of Political Consultants (IAPC) we were guests of the government, although we, of course, paid our own way. We stayed at the King David Hotel, where Abba Iban addressed the group. He clearly laid out what would happen if Israel continued to pursue the "no two-state solution" path that the Likud was then set on. He was prescient. We also were received at the presidential residence and visited the Knesset with Shimon Peres as our guide. Then we toured three of the West Bank settlements, escorted by a member of the Likud Party.

Most of us on the bus were open-minded about the settlements—until we saw them. We visited three kibbutzim. One was owned mostly by wealthy Americans, and to me it looked like Miami East. It was obviously a second-home condo sort of place. The second was a conservative Orthodox community. It had the air of a *shtetl* with its bunker mentality. The third was probably the most typical, a bedroom community filled with young families who commuted to work in Tel Aviv or Jerusalem, and it had the feel of suburbia anywhere. The overwhelming impression I had was "What are these people doing here?" Through the years, as the Likud governments would push to build more settlements in the West Bank and Gaza, the entire operation seemed to me more and more out of joint. For me it almost took on the appearance of two little boys trying to elbow each other off the sidewalk, along with plenty of "I double dare you" words and behavior.

The conference in Israel was wonderful, and we enjoyed being with Matt and Martha Reese as well as the members of IAPC. The mayoral race in Jerusalem was on, and we had dinner one evening with a consultant who was handling one side of the race. The consultant for the opposing side was dining across the room, and there was much friendly banter between the two men. The Mayor of Jerusalem at the time was Teddy Kolak, and he deserves much credit for being fair to his Arab neighbors and building the city into a thriving commercial and tourist center. It was indeed a shining city on a hill, and the yellow sandstone gave it the warm glow of the golden city described in the Bible.

From Tel Aviv we flew to Athens. We toured the Greek peninsula and then went on to London for a day to catch the Concorde. I put on eighteen pounds in six weeks and was glad I had bought a sari in India. That beautiful silk garment was the only thing that fit me so that I could attend the Beaux-Arts Ball in Oklahoma City where Will was an escort for one of the debutantes. Sarah and Henry came down from New York for the affair. I still carry the picture I took of the three of them at the ball.

Chapter 20

FACING REALITY

SARAH AND ED DeLeon had made plans to be married but decided against it. Instead, in 1984 they moved to New York City where Ed began to work on his PhD at NYU. About this time Boots and I became seriously worried about Sarah. Every time we talked to her on the phone, it was like talking to a different person. I was familiar with this pattern, since it is often a sign of someone's being on alcohol or drugs. Her behavior became so concerning that we decided we needed to find out what was happening to her.

We arranged for a formal intervention in case she was using drugs. We met Will and Henry in New York, and with the help of an Oklahoma City psychologist who accompanied us, we participated in an intervention. We discovered she was not addicted to anything but was severely codependent, a mental state some people succumb to when they have grown up in an alcoholic family. They begin to mimic the family member's alcoholic behavior.

The therapist arranged for us to go to Austin, Texas, after the intervention. We would attend a treatment center there for a therapeutic family week. This would give all of us some information about what was going on in the family and give Sarah a chance to see if she wanted more treatment for codependency. It was a fascinating week, one that changed all of our lives. Since I had not gone to a treatment facility before I entered a twelve-step program, this was as close to formal alcohol and drug counseling that I got. Although I had learned a great deal from friends in the AA program and had read books on codependency, it was a revelation to be with other people who were going through the same thing. There were group therapy sessions, one-on-one sessions, and exercises. I was gratified to see that all the children and even Boots seemed to enter into this program with enthusiasm.

The facility occupied a beautiful old house near downtown Austin. The weather was perfect, and I was grateful that my family was finally coming to grips with much of the damage my own addiction had done to our family dynamics. I did some important work there myself and came to a deeper understanding of my own mother and father and what life had been like for them. All our family committed to aftercare, and arrangements were made for them to attend some sessions wherever they lived.

Sarah returned to New York City and to Ed, and she began to improve. The bonus was that her description of her experience at the facility touched a chord with Ed. He realized the impact alcohol had had on his own family and found a place for himself in the Al-Anon program. My only regret about the Austin experience was that we hadn't insisted that Ed go with us. In the end, I suppose it didn't matter, since the message got through anyway.

By now Henry was also in New York City, working for a theater producer who owned an art gallery. In aftercare in New York following his experience in Austin, Henry met his future wife Regina. By then, her father had been sober for almost twenty years and was an alcohol and drug counselor.

Will went away after his own experience with a deepened understanding of the problem of addiction in general and his own habits in particular. Later it would help him to be the main support for one of his best friends who was close to dying at a young age from alcoholism. That friend is still in recovery.

Just after our trip to New York, Boots and I went to California for the 1984 Democratic Convention. While we were in San Francisco, we took the opportunity to visit old friends. During an evening with one couple, Boots described in enthusiastic detail our family-therapy week in Austin. I was gratified that he found it exciting. Our own relationship had become easier, and it was the last time I would hear him discuss the issue. However, our discussion had a surprising result. One of the friends we were talking to later called me about their own addiction. I did not hesitate to suggest a course of action; that person is still in recovery.

Boots and I went to Wisconsin for a couple of weeks after the convention. Another friend of ours had just returned from treatment, and he, his wife, Boots, and I attended a meeting together. I later went to the Al-Anon meeting with Boots and the friend's wife while her husband attended an AA meeting held at the same time. I had been attending Al-Anon during the previous spring because of Sarah's problems. Riding in the car after the meeting, the friend's wife remarked, "Well, I don't want to do that again." I was surprised to hear Boots say, "Neither do I." Later he said to me, "I like myself the way I am, and I don't want to change."

This was an honest statement, and I had to respect it. In all the years we were together he had not changed, except to become more and more closed and distant from those he loved. On the outside he maintained his cordial and almost courtly façade. This was his choice, and there was nothing any of us could do about it.

I think I knew then that his choice would spell the end of our marriage. Almost five years of sobriety had changed me, and I knew continued change would be the only way I could survive without drinking. Without the alcohol and the constant round of anger and remorse, I became much more my own person. I had always been active and independent, but where Boots was concerned, I mostly let him call the tune when I was drinking. Once I became sober, I began to make my own decisions.

❋❋❋

Oklahoma is about as politically unimportant a state as it can be. Democrats generally don't bother with it because they're certain they won't carry it, and Republicans ignore it because they're certain they will. Yet, at a party-nominating convention, every state has its place, and I insisted that Boots become involved if he wanted to return to government service. What he wanted was not going to happen without work. Also, this time I was not going to do the work for him. I was busy trying to run the family trust, which was now our only source of income.

That spring, Boots volunteered to be Oklahoma State Chair for Mondale. He was selected to be a floor manager at the 1984 convention. During that convention, Mondale was nominated along with Geraldine Ferraro, the first woman to run on a major party's ticket. Serving as the floor manager was actually more fun than being a delegate. We had a ball being in the middle of things, visiting with old friends—especially Matt and Martha Reese—and going to parties with my old political consultant pals.

In September, after we returned from the 1984 convention, the fun part was over. As the state chair for Mondale, Boots had to organize the state, and he expected me to help. I told him I would do the Mondale fundraising in Oklahoma for the party, but I would not do the field organizing. Boots hired a woman to do the field work while I did the fundraising. I was told we raised more money in Oklahoma per capita for the party than any state except California. And why not? I had done the house-party fundraising program countless times by then. It was Matt Reese's old "Ten for Ten" or "Ten for the Tenth (Congressional District)" as we called it in Rufus' race. I had been trained by its creator, Matt—the best. I had also used the program in Chuck Robb's Lieutenant Governor's race. The plan consisted of a series of "home parties" along with distributing materials produced by the campaign. The finance chair for the Mondale campaign had been a member of the Virginia State Central Committee.

I was disgusted when I got the material from the Mondale campaign about how to set up the home parties. It was all the same material I used in the Robb campaign. If you are going to rip off something, do it well. I called Matt and complained, saying "at least they could have retyped the stuff." I definitely lack expertise in copyediting. In those days before computers and spell check, they had even reproduced my typos. We had held that conversation earlier in the summer. By the time the fall packets were sent to the states, things were better organized.

I was proud that Oklahoma raised so much money. I was less pleased with the results of my efforts when I presented a bill to the state Democratic Party. I had a verbal agreement with the Executive Director at the time of the campaign that stated that I would charge for my services because I wanted to maintain my status as a professional consultant. In turn, I promised to give the money to the party as a donation, since, as usual, they were in dire straits.

After the campaign I submitted my bill, and it was not a small one; it was for several thousands of dollars. The executive director resigned right after the election. I received a nasty letter from the then-chair of the party asking how dare I charge for my services. I answered that I dared because I was a professional political consultant and that he had permanently lost my services, which would have cost the Democratic Party nothing. I learned a valuable lesson: get it in writing.

I learned another lesson right after the election season. I was the secretary of both the American and the International Association of Political Consultants. All spring and summer I tried to interest someone in helping me coordinate the international meeting in Washington immediately following the election. Boots and I had separated shortly after the election, and my mind was not working well. I took on the entire cost and responsibility by myself and did a terrible job. What I learned was "ask for help, and if you don't get it, keep asking until you do."

That experience was, with one exception—the Supreme Court race in Nevada—the last of my consulting work. Eventually I even dropped my membership in the organization, although I did attend one or two meetings after that.

❋❋❋

Boots and I divorced in 1985 after nearly thirty years of marriage. It was a painful period of my life, and I include the hard years when my mother was ill and when the children were small. I would stand in my office each morning and just feel the pain pervading my body. I felt as though the flesh had been stripped from my bones. Each day brought a kind of self-assessment, reminiscent of the days after the car accident in the 1960s. Each day I would determine whether there had been some slight lessening of pain. The process was glacial.

The only good thing I can say about the divorce was that we came to an almost immediate and amicable split concerning our property. He took all the property he had inherited, and I took all I had inherited. He took his car, I took mine. We divided the books and records in one day. He took his mother's furniture, and I took my mother's. I also received the only assets we owned together: the house in Oklahoma City and the summer house in Wisconsin. I got those assets because we were both in debt, but I had the income needed to meet the payments for the bank loans on the two houses. However, we agreed to divide the time we spent at the lake house because he always loved the place and still wanted to spend time there. That was only fair since we built it mostly with funds from his father's estate. We used the same attorney to draw up the various papers to save money. The decisions were jointly made and simple, but "simple" was still painful.

Chapter 21

ON MY OWN

THE LAST FIVE years of the 1980s were busy for me. There was a lot of wreckage from the marriage to be cleaned up. I began in earnest to attend to business. I paid off the debts Boots and I had accrued, sold the house in Oklahoma City, and bought a condominium near where my sister-in-law Marilyn lived. I paid for it with the proceeds from a second loan I had made to the buyer of the house in McLean. Comfortably settled and having the trust business back to provide a cushion of profitability, I turned my attention to getting my MA in creative writing.

Although I had written a number of articles for the magazine *Campaigns and Elections* and some op-ed pieces for a local paper, my creative writing was limited to the poetry that I had composed as a teenager. I also had a stint in the 1960s preparing adaptations of fairy tales for puppeteers to produce on public television. I had the feeling that I might have sidetracked a career in writing with my involvement in political activity. I especially remembered a conversation I had with a friend in Washington soon after we moved there. I mentioned that I had done the TV scripts, and she said, "I just had lunch with some woman from Baltimore who was starting a television show. I would have asked you to come to lunch too if I had known you had any television experience." The show was *Sesame Street*. How great it would have been to be in on the beginning of such a remarkable and wonderful program. But since that had not happened for me, I decided "better late than never." Thus began my writing career.

I had written one salvageable short story during my years of drinking, a strange and somewhat surreal story about a flight I took from Chicago to Rhinelander, Wisconsin. I was on my way back to the lake from a Panel meeting in Kansas City, and I was exhausted. The woman sitting in front of me was hidden except for a tuft of absolutely white hair. She was wearing a familiar perfume, L'Heure Bleu, the perfume my mother always wore. I suddenly had the fantasy notion that my mother had come back to life and was on the plane. I took some paper out of my briefcase and began to write the story. It was the only survivor of whatever I had written during my drinking years. I had destroyed the rest of the awful fiction I had tried to write during that time. The story about the airplane trip would end up in my first collection of short stories that I had used for my master's thesis. I didn't write anything else that was decent until the summer of 1986. I was driving alone to tour California and stopped in Santa Barbara where I attended a lecture by a Russian author who was at the University of California. I was so inspired, I sat on the grounds of the campus and wrote another story that would join the first in the thesis.

When I returned to Oklahoma, I called Dr. Clifton Warren, who insisted on styling himself Clif. He was the Dean of Arts and Science at the University of Central Oklahoma and I asked him about applying for the master's program in creative writing. It was the only such program in the state that was completely dedicated to writing. He encouraged me to apply. I sent him the manuscripts, my application, and my transcripts, and I was admitted. For the next three years I concentrated on getting the degree. *Wakonta Calendar*, my first set of short stories, was the title of my thesis. Several of them were published in the *New Plains Review*, the university's literary magazine. I also had a chance to interview my old acquaintance N. Scott Momaday for the *Review*. This gave me the occasion to reintroduce myself to him.

When we had lived in McLean, LaDonna Harris had asked to host Scott, who was a Pulitzer Prize–winning Oklahoma author, and Gaye, his wife at that time. Scott came to Washington to help LaDonna raise money for and public awareness of her organization Americans for Indian Opportunity (AIO). This organization helped Native Americans in the cities where they were far from their tribal support systems. Scott and Gaye were delightful guests, and I had the opportunity to renew my acquaintance with Scott in the 1970s, when I helped to coordinate an event in New York City to support AIO. Scott, Boots, and I spent a wonderful evening. After dinner and speeches, we sat in the bar at the Plaza Hotel talking about the various aspects of Native American culture. Scott was a fine writer and a fine scholar, and I learned a great deal listening to him.

The *New Plains Review* was a gorgeous magazine, but like so many publications it could not sustain itself. Clif Warren's ex-wife Gwen was the magazine's editor. She asked me to write a piece for the *Deep Fork Anthology* published by the university. Clif and Gwen were both on my review team for my orals, along with Dr. Lynette Wert, my advisor and the head of the department. Clif and Gwen got into an argument over my stories, so for most of the time they ignored me. I didn't plan it, but this certainly took the edge off any anxiety about my orals. They approved the thesis and awarded me the Geoffrey Bocca Memorial Award for literary excellence shown by a graduate student. Years later I had a novel nominated for a statewide award. At the luncheon for the awardees, I sat next to the head of the writing department at UCO and related the story of the fight that occurred between Clif and his ex at my orals. He said he had heard the story from others.

I will always be grateful for the training and nurturing experience of my classwork at UCO. Under Dr. Wert I wrote many of the episodes that collectively became my first published novel, *A Sky for Arcadia*. Bill Gammel's encouragement sent me back to writing poetry, my first love. The head of the department when I was there had an impressive string of degrees. He lived up to those degrees by making his courses full of outside reading. The final semester, I read twenty-one novels in the process of completing two of his courses. I dropped off my paper on Vladimir Nabokov at his house after graduation as I was on my way out of town to Wisconsin.

UCO, following the tradition begun by Alec Waugh in the 1960s, always had a writer in residence. John Bishop taught film-script writing and gave me my only B grade, which disillusioned me from ever expecting to become a successful writer for the movies. He was a wonderful and practical instructor. Stewart O'Nan began teaching a course in novel writing after I had graduated, but I often went back to take further courses with him. Two books came out of one such encounter: my unpublished second novel and his published novel *A World Away*. These arose from conversations we had as I described to him what it was like to be a child growing up during World War II. I surprised us both by crying in his office. The book you are presently reading had its genesis in the memories I incorporated in that unpublished novel.

ON MY OWN

The 1980s began four decades of travel for me. During the middle of what was supposed to be his senior year in college at the University of North Carolina at Greensboro, Will and I sailed down the Amazon River with Janey and Bob Kennedy in 1986. The highlight of the trip was seeing Halley's Comet in the darkness of the Amazon. The comet made its appearance, but actually it was a disappointment. Its path was far enough away from the earth that it appeared as a fuzzy blob even with binoculars. The trip was spectacular, despite the indistinct comet. Will had always been athletic and good looking. Limbo contests were part of the entertainment on the islands we visited on the way from the mouth of the Amazon to our final destination in Martinique. Will won two of them, and I got a great picture in Tobago when he won.

I have never looked my age. Halfway through the trip I thought about sharing a stateroom with my son. I asked Janey, "People don't think we're a couple, do they?" "Yes," she laughed, "and are they jealous!"

Cruising is not my favorite mode of travel, but it is a great way to cover a lot of ground. Shirley Salzman and I had taken a cruise down the Nile in 1981, and the Kennedys and I sailed the Saint Lawrence river, ending in Montreal at an international conference in 1985. Eventually I went on cruises to New Zealand, the Baltic, and several times to the Caribbean, but I prefer to travel by air or by train when either is available.

I flew alone to Berlin to a meeting of the International Association of Political Consultants and traveled on to Vienna and Rome, where I visited the daughter of friends from Wisconsin and her husband. The husband had a young daughter from his first marriage. She was a shy child and was perfectly behaved when they took her with me to tour Orsini Castle ("orsini" means "bear" in Italian). As we were leaving, she inexplicably started to cry. When we asked what was wrong, she said over and over "orsini." She thought we were going to a zoo to see some bears.

On one of my trips, the Kennedys and I went to Australia for a wonderful three-week visit and traveled as far south as Hobart, Tasmania. We flew to Sydney and went to a performance at the opera house there. When we got to Alice Springs, I remarked, "Looks like Midland, Texas to me." Janey took a picture of me in front of the local women's clinic. At some point during the trip, I got a great picture of Bob Kennedy standing next to a kangaroo. He and Janey were both looking at the camera with their arms crossed as though I had just interrupted their conversation.

We took the Ghana-bound train from Alice Springs to Adelaide. The terrain of central Australia is completely uninhabitable; nothing in the train window grabbed our attention for most of the trip. The place is devoid of people and animals. Janey bravely drove a rental car in Tasmania and had no trouble driving on the "wrong" side of the road. The countryside we saw after we left the north of the island looked like the Cotswolds in England to me. In Hobart we visited craft shops (which Bob insisted on calling "crap" shops) full of wonderful things created by local artists. Just before we left to go back to Sydney and home, we were treated to the sight of a brilliant double rainbow.

At the end of the 1980s, I made a second trip to Israel with members of the Canterbury Choral Society. We went right after Christmas and sang three concerts (along with other American choruses) with the Jerusalem Symphony. The Polish composer Krzysztof Penderecki conducted one concert. The program consisted of his *Seven Last Words*. The performance was awful, and the music was terrible. The orchestra did not seem to know the score, and none of the other choruses were as well-rehearsed as we were. The composer threw a tantrum, and he bellowed at the harpist. However, the music was so atonal that no one could tell the difference; but the audience seemed to love it. We also sang in the church built on the site of the Last Supper at the Cenacle on Mount Zion. In the Church of the Beatitudes by the Sea of Galilee we sang Mozart's Ave Maria for the nuns, and they were entranced; so were we.

The flight back home was unremarkable until we landed in Oklahoma City. Something triggered the oxygen masks to deploy. I have a great picture of me leaning over the seat with all the masks hanging around like Japanese lanterns. While we were in Israel, I lit a candle in the Bethlehem Chapel for my soon-to-be first grandchild. After being in a long-standing relationship, Sarah and Ed were married in 1988. In rapid succession, Henry married Regina McDonald in Amityville, New York, and Will married Courtney Lloyd Wells in Columbia, South Carolina.

In July 1989, Tom was born to Sarah and Ed. Sarah called me in Wisconsin in the middle of the night to say they were on their way to the hospital. The baby had not been due for another week, and I had planned to drive east for the event. Instead, I called the airline, caught the first plane out of Rhinelander, and was in New York City by eleven in the morning. There was plenty of time to hold Sarah's hand since Tom was not born until the next day. By then Boots and Will had showed up to keep Ed company.

It was a joyful time and a perfect way to end the 1980s. The future looked bright. The next six years saw the birth of one grandchild after another. I loved seeing the cousins all in one place: sometimes that place was the Wisconsin lake house. I continued to travel extensively, mostly with Janey and Bob Kennedy, and then with Janey alone after Bob died. A map of my travels would include most of the western United States, China, the Baltic countries, New Zealand, Australia, Eastern Europe, Venezuela, Costa Rica, Mexico, and more.

Janey and I went to China on a tour that included a trip down the Yangtze River after we had seen Peking and the Great Wall. The cruise began with our viewing the spectacular army of ceramic soldiers in Xi'an. We stopped in Wuhan with its lovely museum and ended the river cruise in Shanghai. Janey's grandson had lived and worked there for several years. He was fluent in both Mandarin and the local dialect, and he was a spectacular tour guide.

One trip he arranged was to a lovely town that was preserved as the Chinese had lived for centuries. It reminded me of Williamsburg, Virginia. As we were walking around, Janey's grandson stopped to pet a friendly dog. Then a well-dressed young man with a pretty girl on each arm walked by and looked with contempt at the scene. Speaking in Mandarin he said dismissively to the women, "It's a dog." At this Janey's grandson looked up and smiled. When he said in Mandarin "I know," the young man was embarrassed, and the two girls laughed at him.

During our trip to the Baltic and Russia we had an unexpected chance to see a sight that tourists usually miss. We arranged to have a private guide in St. Petersburg. He was a buoyant fellow and was determined to show us everything. He insisted that we see a lovely Russian Orthodox church outside the city. On the way there we saw St. Petersburg's waste-management site; it was a dump. On one of our last outings together Janey and I spent two glorious weeks on a tall ship sailing the Caribbean. Life was good.

Chapter 22

LOOKING TOWARD A NEW CENTURY

DURING THE 1990s I spent most of my time doing one of five things: I worked, wrote, and traveled; I went to a lot of funerals; and I took part in my last campaign. My generation was then in its late sixties and early seventies. It was a time of life when you may lose many good friends. One of the hardest losses was Bob Kennedy. In addition, Janey and I lost our friend Shirley Robinson. The three of us were known in our circle as the Steel Magnolias. At times I felt like a leaf on a tree watching the other leaves fade and fall. Physically I had never felt better or more energetic.

More important than the losses were the births of my grandchildren Annie, Marshall, and Emily Taliaferro. Since my daughter Sarah's son Tom had been born, Henry's two girls and Will's son were each born, one each year. Then Will and Courtney's daughter Meriwether Taliaferro made her appearance three years after Emily arrived.

For nearly five years, Henry, his first wife Regina, and their girls lived in Oklahoma City. It was heaven for me as grandma but an unhappy time for them. On Saturdays I would take the girls to the Full Circle bookstore for what

Emily called "tory time." The marriage ended, and Regina moved back to California with the girls. However, before leaving they made my sixtieth birthday unforgettable. The girls took me to Chuck E. Cheese, and I had a ball.

I continued to write and completed a second novel and a second collection of short stories. I also wrote an autobiography for my grandchildren that ultimately became this memoir. Once more I was plunged into the world of campaign politics—this time with a difference. I had never worked on a ballot issue except for the one attempt to legalize liquor by the drink when I first moved back to Oklahoma. In one sense, in this last campaign I came full circle. I was once more a volunteer.

In the early 1990s an initiative surfaced to outlaw abortion in Oklahoma. It was patently unconstitutional on its face, but that did not deter its proponents. There was only one man who financed the entire effort. I met him just briefly in the Supreme Court Chamber, but I had great respect for him. He truly believed in what he was doing. I was told he owned a group of nursing homes, and when he sold them to a large corporation, he dedicated one million dollars of his profit to the effort to end legalized abortion in Oklahoma. To my mind, such a person contributes more to society than the constant complainers who never actually do anything, including never voting. Certainly, he was more constructive than the "pro-life" madmen who shoot doctors and blow up medical facilities.

Pam Fleischaker was the first person to be alerted to the anti-abortion petition. As soon as a group of us heard about the initiative, our effort to stop it was underway. We formed a small steering committee, organized ourselves, and began to monitor the drive for the petition. At first the anti-abortion side tried to circulate petitions in churches, thinking they would get plenty of signatures there. Oklahoma may be a supremely conservative state, but our polling data showed that the prevailing attitude toward abortion was about the same as the national average. A majority opposed changing the law. The hard-core anti-abortion vote was about 14%. The most reliable anti-abortion voters are indeed found in the fundamentalist churches and in some Roman Catholic ones, but the minute a voter is faced with a real choice, such as a petition drive or an election, many other motivations come into play.

It soon became clear that some of our opponents' volunteer circulators were not following the stringent rules laid down by the state for ensuring the validity of signatures. Circulating a petition is a tedious and rather complicated business. Each petition must be properly notarized. Each signature, to be valid, must be that of a voter registered in the state. Our opponents soon hired professionals to circulate the petitions. From a public-relations standpoint, we had the advantage if we had to go all the way to a ballot on the issue. We were on the "no" side, and voters are always more likely to vote *no* than *yes* on a ballot issue.

Finally, at the end of the summer our opponents hired a professional group of circulators to finish the job. They filed their petition with barely enough signatures to qualify. We decided, due to the thin margin, to challenge the petition on the grounds that it did not have the required number of valid signatures. Our first help came from the Secretary of State's office, which threw out some petitions that had not been properly notarized or submitted. This invalidated several hundred signatures and brought the total number of signatures tantalizingly close to invalidating the effort.

We put together teams of volunteers to go to each courthouse in all seventy-seven counties of the state. The volunteers were asked to check several indices in these courthouses. In addition, they had to be willing to testify before the Supreme Court. In the large counties such as Tulsa, Oklahoma, and Cleveland, we had to hire people to check signatures. Eventually we had to send hired people to one or two other courthouses as well.

After a year and a half of delay, the hearings started in the state's Supreme Court chamber. The delays came about because our opponents found it much more time-consuming to challenge our challenges than they at first thought would be necessary. Greg Albert, Clerk of the Court, was the hearing examiner, and he was lenient with them. On the surface, it looked as if we had won outright. The opposition, with its highly paid staff and legal team, had done prodigious work, but they had not challenged enough of our objections to thousands of signatures to validate the petition. Then the hearings began, and I learned the vast difference between what you have in your hand and what you can "get into evidence" in court. We had all sorts of trouble, and much of it was our own making. I had begged and pleaded with some of the paralegals I knew to help us put together our document production (evidentiary materials). But I could get no help, and our own lawyers were no help.

We were volunteers, and our only guidance was from the campaign manager, who had done petition campaigns before, for the horse-racing industry and for the Liquor by the Drink campaign. These interests had the funds to hire high-powered law firms. From these lawyers, our manager had learned something about how to go about mounting a challenge.

But we were amateurs. We did stupid things, like number the pages in ink by hand. This caused some discrepancies, which a hand-numbering machine would have obviated. The majority of the challenge sheets from Washington County were somehow lost at the copy center. All the challenges from Comanche County were inadmissible because the checker had missed one of the indices. All of the Seminole County challenges were thrown out because the county clerk there had allowed the checkers to take the poll books home. A portion of the Oklahoma County challenges were inadmissible because the person we hired refused to testify at the last minute. She evidently had some sort of legal problem of her own with the state. We had, of course, already paid her for her work. Some of this was unavoidable, because we could not afford to hire competent staff to get it all done, but the women did yeoman work and were wonderful on the stand.

After the rebuttal, we were very close to winning on the face of it. Greg Albert was quite lenient in allowing the other side's rebuttal. For instance, the law assumes that if you submit several copies of voter-registration cards with the same name as the signer, the signer is a registered voter, regardless of the obvious fact that none of the signatures looked like the signature on the petition. We did not have the money to hire a handwriting expert, and anything less than such testimony was not admissible evidence.

Finally, when we had almost won on the signature challenge, Greg allowed all the signatures that had been thrown out by the Secretary of State to return into the contest as valid. I want to underscore that everything he did had a legal basis. I did say to him at one point, "Greg, it's a good thing I know you so well and like you, because this certainly looks like a payoff." He was rather easygoing and did not take offense. His only comment to me was, "You were 'outlawyered.'" In addition, they spent at least a million dollars, whereas we raised and spent just over $300,000. We had the best counsel we could afford. Our mistake was not to hire the attorney with the most experience in hopes that we could pay the bill. I broke my own rule of always hiring the best counsel I could find.

We lost the signature challenge. But just at that time, the US Supreme Court was hearing another case challenging *Roe v. Wade*—namely *Casey v. Planned Parenthood*. The Oklahoma Supreme Court waited until the high court's decision came down to make their own ruling; they decided *Casey* in favor of Planned Parenthood.

In the meantime, we began to gear up for a fight at the ballot box. Then a majority of the Oklahoma Supreme Court, in a three-way split decision, ruled that the anti-abortion petition, since it was unconstitutional on its face, did not need to be submitted to the people for a vote. We won. My old friend Marian Peter Opala was the Oklahoma Court's Chief Justice, and he wrote the dissenting opinion. He argued that a petition cannot be invalidated on constitutional grounds since it had not yet become a law. Therefore, the process necessarily had to be that the petition must first be submitted to a vote, and only then could any resulting law be challenged.

What I learned from all of this was that in court there is much law and little justice. Justice would have dictated that we would win the challenge to the signature-related part of the petition. They obviously did not have enough valid signatures, and barring this, I always thought Marian was right. How can the constitutionality of a law be challenged if it isn't a law? Still, we won.

Later in the year, a group was put together to write guidelines for the state's Supreme Court to follow regarding signature challenges in the state of Oklahoma. Greg chaired the proceedings. I asked Marian to name me to the committee. As the meetings went on, our lawyers, the other members of the committee, and the legislative staff began to fall away. Finally, only Greg, the two lawyers on the other side of our petition, and I sat down and hammered out some workable rules, using statistics in the initial part of the challenge. That way no one ever again would have to go through the grueling, tedious, inaccurate, and enormously expensive procedure both sides had gone through in the ordeal of checking each signature. As far as I know, there has not been another challenge to test the rules, but we all felt better. And thus ended my active political career.

❦❦❦

I was still busy with my commercial holdings. I sold the original Campus Corner building in Norman and bought a Medical Center in Oklahoma City. Then I sold the shopping center I had purchased in Norman and bought a business building in the industrial section of Oklahoma City. That building once housed an oil company that had gone under during the hard times that hit the oil business in the 1980s. Finally, I sold the Medical Center and bought an abandoned building that belonged to a life-insurance company. It was a wonderful building in mid-town Oklahoma City. By this time, I owned about 125,000 feet of rentable space and had a close relationship with the bank.

In the final years of the 1990s I struggled to renovate these buildings and get them rented. It was not an easy time, emotionally or financially. In 1988, the MT Myers Trust finally expired, and Thurman and I divided all the property into two trusts of our own. To do this, we had to find an attorney. I suggested we hire the attorney who had handled the divorce for Boots and me. We had used the same attorney to save money because we knew exactly how we wanted to divide the property.

I made an appointment to see the attorney and arrived early. My eccentric brother arrived in his turquoise leisure suit and bolo tie. He introduced himself to the young lady at the desk and sat down. She fidgeted. With a worried look on her face, she said, "Sir, you know he doesn't do criminal law."

It was all I could do to hide behind my magazine and burst out laughing. He said in a dignified voice, "I do."

Ultimately, we chose another attorney, my good friend Paul Dudman, who continued to do all my business and estate work. Later, Thurman did not want anything to do with the real estate, so I bought him out. I sold the nice condominium apartment I had moved into when I became divorced. I needed the cash to buy him out and did not want to take on more debt. I rented for a few years and later moved into a charming house on 65th Street in Oklahoma City. The south side of the street backed up to Deep Fork Creek. The moisture from the nearby creek made the trees and lawns especially lush. The houses were all 1950s vintage, one-story ranch-style houses, each one delightfully different. It was a happy home for me.

In the late 1990s I served a third time as president of the Oklahoma City Planned Parenthood affiliate. It was a pleasure to work with the staff, the members of the board, and the new executive director Anita Fream. I always felt appreciated by the people at Planned Parenthood. In January of 1998, they decided to honor Pam Fleischaker and me with the first Frates Award, named for one of our most dedicated supporters. Will came down from Washington to go with me to the dinner. I let him read my speech before I gave it. I followed Pam, a fine writer, to the podium. I talked about what I hoped the affiliate would work for in the future. To underscore the importance of their mission, I spoke for the first time publicly about the rape that occurred when I was eighteen and my decision that suicide would be my solution to any unintended pregnancy. My account reduced the audience to tears, and I was astounded. I never thought of myself as much of a speaker and rarely made formal speeches at all.

However, the focus of the evening really wasn't on our speeches. The story about President Clinton and his dalliance with an intern named Monica Lewinsky had hit the news just before the dinner began. Former Governor George Nigh and his wife Donna were at my table. George was to introduce Pam and me. His first question to my son Will was, "What do you think about the President and the girl?" We had not seen or heard about that matter on television or radio, so we were completely unaware of it. I was as disgusted as everyone else with Clinton's behavior, but I had no awareness of the virulence of the vendetta that would follow.

Bill Clinton occupied the White House from January 20, 1993, to January 20, 2001. The country turned around fiscally during that time, and the Democrats began to act. After a stumbling beginning, foreign policy found its footing; trade policy encouraged what would be called "globalization"; and the government began to take a close look at itself and at Social Security and welfare programs. The United States had budget surpluses and the smallest federal government since Lyndon Johnson's last year in office.

The terrible hate directed at the Clintons in the wake of the Monica Lewinsky affair seemed to be an instance of fear—the fear of change or of losing something you have or of not getting what you want. America had become a greedy, avaricious nation privately and publicly. However, all that is not meant to excuse Bill Clinton's inexcusable behavior. It also does not excuse the tabloid mentality of the press in reporting every dreary detail of Clinton's affair. Nor does it excuse the Republican Party, a party that became unbalanced about its opposition and was dragging out its coverage of the sordid affair. America has truly become a coarse and insensitive country over the past twenty-five years.

The weekend the Starr report that focused on Clinton's behavior came out, I was sitting with Will and Courtney's children, my grandchildren. I got the newspaper early and read it thoroughly. I was incensed, and I immediately sat down and wrote an article for the *Oklahoma Gazette*. It was too long to publish, but I sent it to a number of people. All it did was allow me to vent my anger over the affair.

The Clinton scandal may have occupied the attention of the nation until April 1995 when the unthinkable happened. Sarah and her son Tom were in Oklahoma City for spring break. Tom and his cousins—Henry's girls Annie and Emily—were all playing in my kitchen. The day was sunny and we were preparing to go to the zoo. It was nine o'clock in the morning. Suddenly, the whole house shook, and there was a terrific boom. Emily, who was afraid of thunder, did not seem to notice, nor did the other children. Sarah and I looked at each other and quickly went outside. We couldn't see anything and speculated it was perhaps a plane crash or a gas-line explosion. We went back into the kitchen where the television was tuned to a daytime interview show.

That interview was quickly replaced by a view of the Murrah Federal Building downtown; it had been bombed. Ironically, Judge Murrah was humorous and gentle and a fine federal judge. The Murrah building was beautiful; it was designed by an Oklahoma City architect and was full of art created by Oklahomans, as were many federal offices and daycare centers. We now know that the perpetrator was an American man, Timothy McVeigh, who was soon caught, tried, and finally executed. This was one trial that played out from beginning to end with dignity and some measure of what the United States' system of justice should exemplify. McVeigh had a court trial, and the jury's decision seemed fitting.

I am not an advocate of the death penalty; I think it's futile. It has been demonstrated definitively not to serve as a deterrent. To keep up a practice abandoned by the rest of the civilized world seems like one definition of insanity: doing the same thing over and over again while expecting different results. However, I also understand why Americans want to retain it. When McVeigh was caught and identified, my first reaction was, "Fry him." Attorney General Janet Reno made it clear from the beginning that the Justice Department would seek the death penalty for McVeigh.

At the memorial service for the victims on the Saturday following the bombing, Attorney General Reno entered quietly from a side entrance onto the floor of the State Fair Arena. One could hear a rustle in the audience, and in one movement the entire crowd was on its feet to give her a standing ovation. She stopped for several minutes as though stunned by the reception. She simply stood there to acknowledge the tribute and then went on to take her seat with the survivors from her department.

At the memorial service the Canterbury Choral Society sang, and I sat directly behind the podium from which President Bill Clinton spoke. Despite whatever else he may have done, Clinton's speech at the service was perfect. The governor's wife, with the help of the Philharmonic's executive director, organized the program. Others were involved, of course, but those two created a varied and appropriate tribute that brought the entire city together. It was all accomplished in a necessarily short time.

Since so many Oklahomans held the same populist and libertarian ideas about government that motivated McVeigh, I often wondered if the bomber expected to receive a groundswell of support from people in the state who were following his actions. If so, he was completely mistaken. When I got home after the service I had a call from Will. A group in his office in Washington had watched the service. "Mom," he said, "I was standing there when someone said 'Will, isn't that your mother?' And there you were on CNN."

Chapter 23

RETURNING AND WRITING

AS MUCH AS I loved my friends and my house, Oklahoma City was never a comfortable place for me to live, but the business was there. Finally in 1998 I decided to divide my time between Oklahoma City and the Washington area where I had friends and a residence near Will and Courtney. I sold my house and bought a small condo in Oklahoma City. I then divided my belongings between the Oklahoma City condo and Alexandria, Virginia. I didn't know if I would enjoy living in the DC area again, although I knew I would love being within driving distance of two of my grandchildren and a single flight away from the other three.

Ultimately, it was a good thing that I kept the little apartment in Oklahoma City. In 1996 Thurman was diagnosed with cancer, and a kidney and his ureter were removed. For about two years he had lived relatively comfortably, but by the fall of 1998 he had to leave his beloved house in the mountains of New Mexico and stay in Oklahoma City for treatment. In 1999 he lived the last three months of his life with me. It was a difficult time, but he and I had many wonderful conversations. One of the last things he said to me was how much he appreciated my taking care of him. I was glad to do it. His ex-wife Marilyn did more than her share of helping him through his medical difficulties. She didn't need to do so, since they had by then been divorced for more than twenty-five years, but she did it without complaint. She was one of the earth's truly good people. All three of their daughters took turns coming to Oklahoma City to be with their father and to help with his care, Valerie left her two teenage sons, and Margo took leave from her job with an international firm. Adrian drove in almost weekly from Elk City.

Thurman died on April 23, 1999, three days before my birthday. We had a wake and a birthday party on Thursday and a small memorial service for him on Friday. The mourners were confused by the gales of laughter coming from the family room where we waited for the service to begin. One of my friends who knew all of us well said, "I knew what you were doing. You were telling Thurman stories." She was right. My brother was one of those lovable eccentrics only the British and their own families can truly appreciate.

A year later I had my own battle, with breast cancer. For years I had been monitored closely, because I had had a number of cysts removed for biopsy; the first was done when I was in college. In January 2000, the results came back positive. I was extremely lucky to get by with a minimum of surgery. I had the surgery in Oklahoma City since I had not yet found doctors in the Washington area. As soon as I was strong enough, I went back to Alexandria. Sarah came down from Boston to stay with me for more than a week, and I began the eight-week series of radiation treatments at Alexandria Hospital. I am grateful to have found a wonderful team of doctors who still look after my welfare meticulously.

My reaction to the radiation treatments was minimal, and as the shock of being told I had cancer began to fade, I packed it away with all of the other losses in my life. I now think of myself as a survivor, not as a victim. I learned to live with the fear, which becomes its strongest every six months when I have a mammogram. My gratitude was overwhelming when I walked with all my sisters in pink shirts at the Susan G. Komen Walk on the Mall in Washington. Now, at my age, I no longer need to do the mammograms. If there is a recurrence, it's up to fate.

Before and after my cancer episode, I continued to travel and be active in my community. I went to the office of the Planned Parenthood of the Washington area and volunteered. It was my pleasure to once more serve on a Planned Parenthood board. I also served as chair of its political action division and as co-chair of the fundraising committee to build their magnificent new clinic in northeast Washington. Life in Washington was engaging and interesting, and I looked forward to what I hoped would be calm years of retirement.

My permanent relocation to the East Coast took five years. I kept the small apartment in Oklahoma City and commuted for three or four weeks between the two cities. This allowed me to establish a life in the Washington area with two old friends and to oversee the business. Jennie kept things going while I was away, and Tony was quite capable of managing the buildings with me because I could always be reached by a phone call in case of an emergency.

Old Town Alexandria was within walking distance for most things, and the Metro station was within driving distance, so I could move around the city with ease. The new millennium began with George W. Bush's election and the trauma of 9/11. That fateful day, I returned from my morning walk along the Potomac and heard my telephone ringing. It was my niece Adrian in Oklahoma City.

"Are you alright?" she asked.

"Sure, why?"

"Turn on the television," was all she said and hung up.

I turned on the set just in time to see the second tower hit. The rest of the day I spent mesmerized by the events that unfolded as I had done with the bombing of the Murrah Building in Oklahoma City. I had the doors to the patio open and realized I could smell smoke from the Pentagon.

Later I would learn that the collapse of the World Trade Center's twin towers had taken the lives of two young men who were sons of good friends from Oklahoma City. Both boys had established careers in New York City. I returned to Oklahoma for the funeral of one of them. For those of us old enough to remember the shock of Pearl Harbor, 9/11 brought back vivid memories.

In Virginia I enjoyed being where my son Will and his wife Courtney were. Once again, I could be "Grandma" to Marshall and Meriwether, their children. I didn't get to do as much as I liked with them because they soon moved from Arlington to Loudoun County Virginia, west of DC. Sarah and her son Tom visited often from Boston, and they had even helped me celebrate New Years 2000.

My children talked me into adding to my personal real estate by purchasing a small condo at Wintergreen, a ski resort in the Blue Ridge mountains. "Mrs. Taliaferro of Oklahoma City, Alexandria; Hazelhurst, Wisconsin; and Wintergreen," daughter-in-law Courtney teased. They enjoyed the weekends they spent there, and I used it as a writing retreat.

I did much less overseas travel but continued to see the United States. In the spring of 2005, Lynda Robb called me and invited me and our mutual good friend, Sarah Gayle Randolph, to go with her to the Johnson Ranch. She wanted us to go for a visit while Mrs. Johnson was still alive, because when she was gone the entire premises would be owned and managed by the Park Service. Everything in the house at the time of her death would belong to the movement and the girls could not remove anything from the house or have any say over what was done there.

Sarah Gayle and I flew to Austin where we had dinner with my two older nieces Valerie and Margo and their husbands. The following day Lynda picked us up and drove us to the ranch. It was early summer and lovely weather. When I walked in it felt like home. The house was built about the same time my parents built the house in Oklahoma City, and both reflected the "ranch style." Most of the rooms were on the first floor where the Johnsons spent their time. The second-floor bedrooms were for guests or visiting family. My room had charming Victorian furniture that I believe once belonged to Lynda's grandmother. While the lower floor reflected the mix of mid-century modern, classic American and simply comfortable furniture favored in the 1950s, my bedroom reflected an updated Early American flavor.

On the second floor was a room I would call either a sun porch or loggia. What I remember best were the hand-drawn pictures each of the Johnson girls had done as children depicting their days at their beloved Camp Mystic.

Lynda took us to view the Wildflower Center where the lavender was in full bloom. Then we went to what was the largest flea market I had ever been to. There were several steel buildings of stuff. We rummaged about for furniture for Lynda's daughter, Katherine, who lived and practiced law in Austin and had just bought her first house. We had great fun until the heat soared up into the 90s at least.

Most of my time since 2000 has been occupied by writing. Although I completed the manuscripts for my novel *A Sky for Arcadia* and a first draft of *Virgin Hall* in the 1990s, I published nothing. I did continue to add to my short-story collection and to write poetry, often prompted by a group of poet friends in Wisconsin. We still meet once a month, and together we published an anthology, calling ourselves the Paper Birch Poets. Whether they were or were not published, this fellowship of poets has continued to be a writing joy, and the advent of Zoom has made it possible for me to participate each month.

Technology has made a difference; I am in Virginia, one member is in North Carolina, and a third is in Illinois. We are all members of the Wisconsin Fellowship of Poets or WFOP, an organized and active group. The group publishes a calendar each year and is generous in making its acceptances. We also have contests, and though I rarely enter, I did receive an honorable mention for one poem.

For several summers, I attended writing retreats at The Clearing, a lovely and private retreat in Door County, Wisconsin. The cottages are comfortable, the lodge is inviting, and the food is wonderful. I went in spring when the lady slippers and trillium were in bloom. After attending several workshops there, I completed and self-published "Breaking the Surface," my chapbook of poetry.

Still, none of my fiction had been close to printer's ink except for the few stories that were published in *The Northern Virginia Review*. There were near misses. When I was still in graduate school, I entered a Redbook short-story contest back when magazines still published stories, and I received a letter from the fiction editor. Of the thousands of submissions they received, mine ranked nineteenth. I also received a letter from one member of the editorial staff that told me about my ranking, complimented my writing, and encouraged me to submit more stories.

With two kids in New York at the time, I took the opportunity when I was there to have tea with the editor and subsequently sent another story to her that was accepted. However, a senior editor pulled it. The editor then asked me to write a Christmas story that the senior editor turned down, saying it was "too dark" to publish. I gave up rather than continuing to submit any more of my stories.

By the time I settled in Washington, I was ready to concentrate on writing and publishing. When I could find neither agent nor publisher, I decided to self-publish my first novel. Print-on-demand self-publishing was new. I chose Xlibris. Founded in 1997, Xlibris Publishing was one of the first ventures into private publishing that was professional and more than a vanity press. I contacted them and contracted to have *A Sky for Arcadia* published.

I proceeded to make every conceivable mistake. Sarah created a wonderful jacket for the book, meticulously copyedited my manuscript, and even formatted it for printing. (She made her living as a graphic designer.) Then I promptly sent the wrong manuscript file to the publisher. Instead of going back to my daughter, since she was busy then as an employed single mother in another city, I thought, "I'll do it. After all, surely the spellcheck function has taken care of most of the problems, and the publisher takes care of layout."

The paper galleys sent back to me were a disaster. Foolishly, I took red pen in hand and did a ton of editing and correcting. I discovered I was the world's worst copy editor when the book came out. It was so bad that I had Xlibris do a second printing after their copy editor cleaned things up. This all ended up as "good news, bad news." The bad news was that the final edition of the book still contained several mistakes, and it was hard for me to read because it exposed some bad writing habits I had acquired over the years. Later, wonderful editors called them to my attention. The good news was that the novel was a finalist in the Library of Congress' Center for the Book program, which selects titles from each state. It also sold well—phenomenally well I was to discover. The last royalty check I received from my present publisher was for $16.89.

In response to this failure to be a "best seller" and the only thing that keeps me from thinking I'm just a lousy writer is the consolation that I always get great reviews and feedback from my few readers. That is enough encouragement to keep my literary ego going. In truth, the only reason my first book sold well was because I was still young enough in my seventies to do the hard work of personal marketing. Since the novel has to do with addiction and a woman's first year in recovery, I took copies to a convention of addiction councilors. One of them evidently read it at night during the conference. "I like your story," she said. Since people in recovery refer to the events of their lives as "their story," I immediately answered, "Oh, it's not *my* story. It's all fiction." She burst into laughter and said "Well, if it's not your story, who wrote it?"

I would discover that at least one treatment center bought the book in bulk to give to the women who graduated. I also took a box of the books to the International Convention of Alcoholics Anonymous in San Antonio in 2010. Fortunately, a friend went with me to run my booth, because it was beastly hot and we were suffering from the remnants of a hurricane. The place was like a sauna, and our booth was outside. I came close to having heat stroke one afternoon; I went to the hotel, drank lots of water, and lay down in the darkened room until I felt normal again.

By this time Amazon was in the self-publishing business. I considered it, but then an old friend from McLean called and said she and a friend were starting a publishing venture and was I interested. I said "yes" and signed a contract with them. We eventually fell out, sad to say, and I terminated the contract. Even so, their editorial help made the book much stronger. Their help was crucial, because of all my books *Virgin Hall* took the greatest amount of time to complete. *A Sky for Arcadia* was essentially written when I was still in graduate school. There was a long period in the 1980s when I did not write, but I continued to work on the manuscript intermittently. By the time *Virgin Hall* was finally published, it had gone through at least four iterations. It began as a short story when I was in school. I liked the characters so much that I thought they needed their own book. I wrote the first draft in the third person; it didn't work. I went back and rewrote it in the first person. With the first publisher I did considerable rewriting and reorganizing and went so far as to drop some characters.

At this point, Amazon offered Create Space as an affordable and convenient print-on-demand publishing house. Create Space is now called KDP. *Virgin Hall* was published by them, as was my second collection of short stories *CityScapes*. My first collection was also my master's thesis.

This second collection is my favorite of everything I have written. I find it to be the most polished and literary example of my work, even though my first collection, *Wakonta Calendar*, won the Bocca prize for graduate writing. I had started writing many of the stories in *CityScapes* during the 1990s when two of my children and their spouses were living in New York City. It started in a fit of pique. I was frustrated at being unable to find an agent or an editor and suspected that because I was living in Oklahoma City I was at a disadvantage. I apparently share some of my fellow Oklahomans' paranoia about how the state is viewed, and I thought, "Well, I can write about New York City. I'm always there." Consequently, all of the stories are tied in some way to New York with one exception, a story about race relations. I submitted the first story in the collection to the O'Henry contest, and although I received no prize, I did get a lovely letter. If I had been smart, I would have resubmitted it the following year.

That story was later reprinted in a textbook written and edited by a friend from Alexandria. Her textbooks were designed for critical reading, and she used it in the book's appendix for her students to read and discuss because it deals ambiguously with suicide and murder. This story, along with another from the collection, won first prize from *The Northern Virginia Review*. Money prizes are nice.

The inspiration for the final story I wrote for *CityScapes* came to me in a way I had never before experienced. I was in Wisconsin after putting the collection of stories in the order I wanted. I went to bed fussing at myself. "It's too short. There has to be one more story." I was completely out of ideas. The next morning, I awoke, and the entire story was complete in my imagination. I've never had that sort of editorial help since.

Then along came COVID and the lockdown it caused. By this time I had moved from Alexandria to Leesburg, Virginia, to be closer to the children. I knew that if I was isolated in my apartment with only the television, I would go mad. On my computer was the first chapter of a historical romance novel. Sarah and I, both devotees of Jane Austen, indulged ourselves over the years reading Georgette Heyer and subsequent historical-romance authors. I dug out the chapter and set to work. It took me only about three months to complete a decent first draft.

By chance, a friend of Courtney who had just finished a novel put me in touch with a British woman who edited books and lived only about a mile from me. I was delighted to find someone with a British background who could look over my work since I had not been to England in years. She was wonderful and thorough. We spent an hour on the phone calculating how long it would take to get from London to Wells in Somerset by coach. At one point she called me and said, "I've looked and looked for Tinston in Cornwall, and I can't find it. Did you make the village up?" I had invented the small town the heroine returns to.

I looked up romance publishers and took the easy way out. Decadent Publishing LLC put out a call. I did submit the manuscript to several other publishers to no avail, but the response from Decadent was immediate. Despite its rather lurid appearance, this publishing house is wonderfully professional, and it assigned me to a fabulous editor who vastly improved my writing. Before I signed the contract, I had an attorney who was the son of a friend look it over. He called me and said, "Do you know what kind of publisher this is?"

"I do," I answered.

My son Will asked me the same question and received the same answer. Both Will and Henry found it hilarious that Mom in her eighties was writing smutty books.

I am grateful to Decadent for publishing both *A Reasonable Lady* and *An Unreasonable Daughter*. Sadly, they declined a third book in the intended trilogy because the first did not sell well enough. Later I would discover that readers had an aversion to anything called "romance," until I explained that the books were closer to Jane Austen's novels than to *Fifty Shades of Grey*. I will say that undertaking these projects kept me sane all through the pandemic.

After finishing the third romance, I was tired of writing. The only thing left on my computer was the manuscript of a novel I had written when I still lived in Oklahoma City. It was set in the final months of World War II and was highly personal. I pulled all sorts of scenes from my memories and created a family much like my own when I was growing up with my parents and their two other children. At one point when I was writing it my brother called. He was never close to my mother, while I was close to both my parents.

"How's the book about the bitch coming?" he asked.

"Fine," I said. I finished the manuscript and put it away. One of my professors said that many authors have a turkey in the closet they never publish but will pick at occasionally. I had real doubts about the project but decided to give it a try. With the help of another writer friend, I contacted a book coach. When I first started writing, I hadn't known such a profession existed. I contacted her and said, "I don't really need a coach, I've already written and published five books. But I do need an editor. Can you look this thing over?"

She did, and we mutually agreed that the plot was so flawed it couldn't be salvaged. During the conversation I mentioned that many of the incidents in the book could be found in a memoir I had finished in 2000 for my children and grandchildren. She asked if she could look it over, and I sent it along. "You need to publish this," was her conclusion this time. She put me in touch with Bold Story Press, and the book you are now reading is the result.

While I was trying to become a published author, I continued to run the trust. Several things happened at one time to make me decide to give up the management of the properties. Early one morning in August 2005 the phone rang. I answered, and Henry said "Hi, Mom, I'm in Las Vegas." After the briefest of pauses he added, "And I got married." This was my introduction to my new daughter-in-law Kathryn LaBach. By then, Henry had been divorced for about ten years, and Kathryn, who was twelve years younger, had never married. She was an attorney who worked for the government as a bank examiner, and they had met at their Episcopal church in Beverly Hills where both had been active.

Their friends in the church's congregation were disappointed that they had eloped instead of having a ceremony, and so was I. The following summer they had a "blessing" ceremony at the church to satisfy us all. The couple made all the plans for the event, and I hosted the rehearsal dinner at an Italian restaurant the night before.

Henry's daughters, Annie and Emily, were attendants for the ceremony. The girls looked lovely in black dresses and carried huge bouquets of sunflowers. Kathryn, a native of Overland Park, Kansas, loved the state flower. After the ceremony everyone went to a restaurant for burgers, fries, and shakes.

Henry and Kathryn continued at their jobs until their daughter Caroline was born in April 2007. They wanted to leave Los Angeles. Kathryn didn't want to raise a child there, and Henry's girls had moved with their mother to Alabama, so he had nothing to keep him in LA. I thought it was a perfect solution to hire him to run the trust. In late 2006 I became nervous about the commercial real estate market. I hasten to say this was not because I was clairvoyant or even smart. It was a feeling, and I began losing sleep at night thinking about how much money I owed the bank. I called my wonderful broker Tim Strange, who helped me keep my buildings full of tenants. Tim was just setting up his own brokerage firm. He said to me, "Put the buildings on the market, please." By February 2007, he had sold every foot of commercial real estate that I owned and happily pocketed his fees.

He and I did very well just before the oncoming real estate crash. I had not paid any capital gains taxes on the properties through the years, preferring to do a "like-kind exchange," an arrangement whereby I purchased another property using the proceeds from the sale within three months. This time I paid the taxes, so I was free and clear of bank loans for the first time in twenty years.

In 2004 Sarah and Tom moved from Boston to be closer to Will and me and so that Tom could be near Ed, his dad, who had relocated to Maryland. In 2004 I sold the properties in Alexandria and Wintergreen and bought a condo in Loudon County, Virginia, close to both Will and Sarah and their families.

Henry and Kathryn made plans to move to Kansas City, Kansas. They had no desire to move to Oklahoma City, and Kathryn's parents were in Overland Park, Kansas. By that time I was ready to get out of the management business even though the trust remained in force. This meant everything I owned, including the condos and mineral rights, was in the trust and solely in my name.

Henry took a commercial real estate course and joined a firm that was connected with Tim Strange's firm. He worked for them while he became familiar with the trust. He and Kathryn rented a house and moved from Los Angeles while I closed up shop in Oklahoma City and moved the office to Kansas City. The only thing I hated was leaving my employees, Jennie and Tony. Jennie had seen me through more than twenty years of making decisions, and Tony had made the burden of building management easy for me. After the real estate market had cooled off somewhat, Henry and I went building hopping. We found a property we still own, and he took over management of everything. We have a regular family remote call about things, but the responsibility is all his. After that, I made one more major decision about my estate. The oil business was again booming, and I had more money than I needed.

Henry was getting along, but he had only a salary from the trust, which meant Kathryn had to work while she had an infant to take care of. Her mother did a major part of providing care for Caroline. Sarah was scraping by in her job as a graphic artist who designed packaging and was a single mother. She was well paid, but she was downsized once and then again. Will, as a partner in Greer, Margolis, Mitchell, Burns, an advertising firm, was secure in his job. None of my children ever asked for or received money from me. Since leaving college they have made their own way in the world.

I decided to contact Paul Dudman, my long-time attorney in Oklahoma City, and to make plans to transfer everything except the Virginia condo and my car into limited liability corporations (LLCs). One LLC contained the oil properties and real estate, another one held the house in Wisconsin in common, and a third was an insurance trust I had set up for my children years earlier. Each of us received one quarter of the shares in the LLCs that contained the mineral interests and real estate.

This additional income made it possible for Kathryn to quit work. For Sarah it meant she could "stop filling up landfills and do something positive." She went back to school at George Washington University and earned a master's degree in teaching children with emotional disabilities. She adored her students and teaching. I sat back and enjoyed the neatness of my life with no responsibilities. This was not destined to last.

Chapter 24

ANNUS HORRIBILIS

IN 1992, THE year Windsor Castle burned, Queen Elizabeth dubbed the year "annus horribilis" ("horrible year" in Latin). Many families go through a time of seemingly endless trauma that lasts a year or two. Ours began in the fall of 2011 when Henry was diagnosed with prostate cancer. He was fortunate to have effective treatment and surgery and is now well.

In January 2012, I was diagnosed with the beginnings of mutable myeloma. Although it gave me a scare, the disease has been manageable; it is progressing slowly, and the only treatment to date has been to receive occasional iron infusions to take care of the anemia. In March of that year I got a call from Sarah about Will's son. She said, "Mom, Tom and I are on our way to Fairfax Hospital. Marshall has had an accident."

"Automobile?" was my first question.

"No, skateboard, but it's bad. He's in the trauma unit."

We dashed to the hospital, and when I got there, I found that police were investigating the incident. Marshall had been on a skateboard, but an automobile was involved. When I arrived at the hospital, Marshall's best friend Brian was sitting outside on the curb sobbing. I put my arms around him and, by listening to him and the policeman, I managed to piece together that Marshall had tried to "hook a ride" by hanging onto the back of the car Brian was driving. Marshall lost control, which resulted in his severe head injury. There were no charges, and the policeman said to me that it was just "boys being boys."

Marshall spent from mid-March until after his twenty-first birthday on May Day in the hospital's intense-care unit. We all visited daily, even though we rarely saw him because only one visitor was allowed, and that visit was restricted to a limited amount of time. After months of Marshall's receiving excellent care at Inova Fairfax Hospital, his parents' devoted attention, and his mother's oversight of his recovery, he survived. At one point he was in a rehab facility in Charlottesville, VA. I remember the first sound I heard him make after the accident; he was watching a hockey game and laughed.

We had no idea how much of his faculties he would recover. Today he still suffers from a dropped foot and slight impediments but nothing more than someone who might have suffered a slight stroke. Whatever cognitive disability remains has not kept him from full employment. Best of all, he's the father of Miss Anne Wells Taliaferro, who delights us all.

Marshall was still in rehab when I left for Wisconsin. During my stay I drove from the lake house into Stillwater, Minnesota, to help nurse my friend Toni through the final stages of lung cancer. She was on oxygen and restless, so I slept in the bedroom on the lower floor of her split-level home. I was just falling asleep when my cell phone rang. It was Will. He said, "Mom, I'm on my way to Fairfax Hospital. Sarah had a seizure, and they did a CT at Loudoun Hospital. She has a brain tumor." I had a flashback to Sarah's call about Marshall.

I did not have the luxury of denial. Eight years ago I had gone through this experience with my dear sister-in-law Marilyn. I knew only too well the progression and the outcome. I could hear Toni walking around above me, dragging her oxygen tank. I ran up the stairs crying, and fell into her arms. I had come to be a comfort to her, and she became a comfort to me.

My drive back to Wisconsin to leave the car and fly to Virginia began early in the morning. In the half-light that left everything in gray scale without color, all I could think of was sitting at the kitchen table shortly after Sarah was born, nursing her, and savoring being completely alone in the silence with this beautiful baby.

In the years since Sarah was diagnosed, several notable people and one close friend have died from glioma. In each case I heard the news and began calculating the months. I immediately recalled that first there is the surgery, when doctors will excise what they can. Then comes the radiation, six to eight weeks daily except on weekends. Later there are typically some good weeks or months before the chemo really takes hold and symptoms begin to show, such as falling. I calculate how long it will be until death happens.

Sarah's care fell to me and to her twenty-four-year-old son Tom, who lived with her. He had the hardest part because they lived in a three-story townhouse, and as the disease progressed there was a lot of physical labor involved in getting her up and down stairs and finally in and out of bed. He and I spent some time getting her to the National Institutes of Health in Bethesda, Maryland. Her oncologist put her in a study there. I looked up the protocol, and it was for glioma. Technically, she was diagnosed with astrocytoma, so there seemed to be a distinction without a difference, at least in treatment and outcome. The bright spot was that her ex-husband Ed would come and sit with Tom and me, and we would take her out to lunch. At one such lunch we were joined by my cousin's daughter, a young woman whose husband was a cardiologist at the National Institutes of Health (NIH).

Sarah continued to teach until sometime in April. When she could no longer handle the classroom, Loudoun County Schools moved her to an administrative job that she kept until she began to fall too much, and then they gave her retirement. Sarah, Tom, and I did spend some time at the lake. He was able to get her on and off the airplane. Soon after they left, she was back in the hospital, so I returned to Virginia. Her hospital stay was followed by two stints in rehab. I would go be with her in the morning, and Tom would be with her in the afternoon. She made little progress, and finally the insurance ran out for rehab.

I went desperately looking for a facility that provided managed care. Finally, the director of the one facility I would have put her in said, "We are full and can't take her, why don't you try the old place by the hospital?" That facility had the same name as a much larger national chain, but I demurred because it wasn't close by. "Oh, no," she informed me, "The one here in town is the original hospital with managed care."

Sarah was placed in a charming Victorian house with a two-story wing that contained hospital rooms. The residents ate together downstairs in a lovely dining room. There was a large living room and a parlor where Sarah and I sat and watched movies such as *Casablanca*. The staff was attentive and kind to the patients. In addition, hospice personnel came and worked with Tom to make all the necessary arrangements.

On a Thursday morning in November, I was in the shower and had the sudden urge to get out, get dressed, and get to the care facility. As I walked in, the little nurse who had taken special care of Sarah met me at the bottom of the stairs. My beautiful fifty-six-year-old daughter was gone. Friends who were in recovery or were from my Episcopal church walked with me step by step through the entire experience. To deal with it, I wrote a book titled *Awake at First Light*. It was not published; it was therapy.

The aftermath had one other terrible outcome. Sarah's son Tom had a psychotic episode. Fortunately, he was able to be at his father Ed's house for a few months after Sarah died. Ed had experience with this sort of condition in his family and knew just how to handle it. He, his wife Julie, and I have seen Tom through a couple of episodes since, but he has made a life for himself, much of it with friends who play music.

He continued to live in Sarah's house until the spring of 2023 when Tom, Ed, and I got rid of everything except what Tom needed for an apartment. I watched as the auctioneer took things that belonged originally to my mother, my grandmother, and my mother-in-law. I sold the Taliaferro family's silver and china. I went through everything and picked out a few lovely, signed pieces-of-art glass that Sarah had purchased and set them aside for Tom to keep. Luckily, he wanted to keep all the paintings, including the ones Sarah had done. He put them and a few other things in storage. Will took the family pictures, and I sent Henry a couple of his grandmother's things that he wanted. I found I could do the grueling task and not obsess over things.

When I took a number of items to an antique dealer in Falls Church, Virginia, I was given one of the best pieces of advice I ever received. I was looking at a figurine my grandmother had given my mother. The owner smiled at me, and said, "If something speaks to you, keep it. Otherwise let it go." I kept the figurine.

The years since have not been all loss or without joy. My six grandchildren have grown to maturity. Sarah's son, Tom, has a townhouse near us in Leesburg. Henry's three girls are spread from coast to coast. Annie married Howard Sider, and they live in Durham, North Carolina, where she teaches high school chemistry. Emily returned to Burbank, California, where she was born and works in HR. Caroline is off to her freshman year at the University of Kansas. Will's two live close to us. Meriwether works in corporate administration. She married her high school sweetheart, Sierra Kelly. Sierra, who was born in far southwestern Virginia but lived elsewhere, has helped me understand the fears and motivations of people who do not share her political views or mine. Marshall and Sarah Bartkowski presented us with the spectacular Miss Anne Wells Taliaferro, who loves kindergarten.

Chapter 25

A FINAL DECISION

THE ISOLATION IMPOSED by COVID and the loss of my dear cat Grace forced me to realize although I was comfortable in the condo, I was lonely. This was compounded by the illness of my friend Sean Holly. Sean and I had lunched together at least twice a week for years. I have a picture of us that was taken at my eighty-fifth birthday party, and I threw a party for him on his ninetieth. By then driving had become impossible for him, so I often drove out to West Virginia where he lived and took him to lunch.

Sean lived in a three-story townhouse and resisted all the efforts of his children to get him to move. I even tried finding him a place, to no avail. By the beginning of 2023, he began to fall and finally ended up in Inova Loudoun Hospital. His sons packed his belongings and moved him to an apartment in the independent-living part of a retirement community that was only about a mile from where I lived. When he was released from the hospital I went to see him at the retirement home.

The place was sunny, and he had an apartment that looked out on nothing but trees. The staff was caring, and people were friendly. I couldn't help admonishing him and said "You should have come here five years ago. And I wouldn't have had to drive so far." Unfortunately, his stay at the hospital revealed that he had an advanced case of lung cancer. He was in the apartment for only a few months before he was transferred to the assisted-living part of the facility. I went to see him there before I left for Wisconsin. We spoke over FaceTime late in the summer so I could say goodbye.

I kept thinking about the retirement home I visited when I took Courtney with me to an "introductory tea" and pored over apartment floor plans. Then I put my name on the list in the fall of 2023, planning to move there sometime in the spring of the following year. But the perfect apartment "with trees" became available in November. I spent two months sorting through twenty years of accumulation in my condo. Many of the things I got rid of were from my mother and grandmother, but I was able to let go of them with the same efficiency I had learned when I closed Sarah's house.

I did have a friend, a self-proclaimed "neatnik," help me with clothes; she was wonderful. It only took a morning before I had neat piles of "out," "keep," and "to Wisconsin." With the help of several of my friends from my women's recovery group, along with my children and grandchildren, I was in my new apartment by mid-January. I was relieved to have done this before I needed to put my children through what Sean's children had gone through.

Life here is just right for me at my age. I still occasionally cook since I have a full kitchen in independent living, but it is nice not to have to do it. In addition, I found a compatible group of friends and a helpful staff. Soon after I moved in, they arranged a book signing at Barnes & Noble when my second romance was published. I can't believe I look forward to bingo on Monday night. Maybe the fact that it is organized by the residents and we use real money has something to do with its attraction. Best of all, I don't own one piece of real estate, with the exception of my quarter of the lake house, and the office takes care of that.

One other event changed my lifestyle. Several months after I moved, I went to Reston to see the condo my granddaughter Meriwether and her spouse Sierra had just rented. Being unfamiliar with the route I made a mistake, and in trying to correct it I took out a sign. It did considerable damage to the front of my car and to my self-confidence. The repaired auto went to Marshall, along with my car keys.

This was a lot of freedom to give up, but friends pick me up for events, and there is a driver here on Mondays and Wednesdays to take me to medical appointments. I have remained active with St. Gabriel's Episcopal Church, a remarkable little parish that's more than half Latino. We have no church building but meet in the cafeteria of a local middle school. The parish runs an enrichment school for Hispanic youth and has a ministry at the Texas border. It participated during COVID with Catholic Charities and the county to distribute hundreds of thousands of dollars in rental assistance. It also bagged food that was donated by the local food pantry to be delivered during the pandemic to families who could not get out. At the peak of COVID it served some eighty families. All this was run and coordinated by Father Daniel Velez-Rivera along with volunteers from the parish from a 200-square-foot office that was donated by the local Episcopal church.

I recently acquired a caramel-colored male cat named Mochi. He quickly took over the apartment and left me a small space of my own. We are quite content with each other. My life has not been smooth, but it has been interesting. I wouldn't have missed the ride for anything.

EPILOGUE

IN THESE YEARS after my activity with politics and Planned Parenthood, my participation has been limited to occasionally giving advice when asked and writing checks.

My interest in public life has continued. I remember right after Ronald Reagan was elected in 1980 attending the meeting of the American Associations of Political Consultants. We partnered with something like the Public Affairs Council, so it was a major occasion. I sat in the auditorium and on the stage were some of Reagan's newly appointed cabinet members who spoke to us. I particularly remember listening to Ed Meese.

"Oh, God," I thought, "these guys know what they are doing." I thought this with a sense of foreboding and continued to watch as big business made its power felt in the government, and "trickle down" economics took hold.

Clinton's election was a short and not completely satisfying two terms. After George W. Bush was elected I had the distinct feeling that everything I had worked so hard for was beginning to unspool. I was especially unnerved by the Supreme Court's decision in the Citizens United case. I knew all too well how devastating it would be to elections.

EPILOGUE

In addition, the rise of obstructionists in Congress made governing for either party nearly impossible.

As encouraging as Obama's eight years were, the quick unraveling in the next four was a blow for progressives. Biden's administration was only an encouraging stopgap. At least under his guidance, for a few years the government spent its money on people rather than business organizations. Both the Affordable Care Act under Obama and the CHIPS and Science Act and Infrastructure bill under Biden were faint glimmers of the vision my generation, led by President John F. Kennedy, had for our nation. Our hope is in history. Times change.

As I observe America now, I am brought full circle to the Civil War statues of those impossibly young men.

They should change faces. Appomattox should wear the eager expression of the soldier in South Bend. The Northern soldier ought to wear the dejected look of defeat.

It is a bitter thing to win the wars and lose the peace. Perhaps we must lose the peace in order to appreciate the victories.

—Janet Taliaferro
November 2025

ACKNOWLEDGMENTS

MY DEEPEST THANKS to Emily Barrosse and her highly professional team at Bold Story Press. They shepherded me through the entire process of publishing this book with patience and good humor. My editor, Karen Gulliver, oversaw the rewriting of a mound of raw material and helped make sense of it to produce a book with some coherence. I have used Word for as long as it has been around, but Jocelyn Kwiatkowski saved me more than once from doing something disastrous with the newest version. I am grateful to the entire crew from first draft, through the cover creation, to marketing assistance.

Writers know the process of producing a book is impossible without the aid of editors and readers. Native New Yorker Arnie Friedman led me through pulling together CitiScapes and kept me from geographical errors. I want to acknowledge Caroline Hedges and particularly Laura Garland who improved my writing substantially while helping with my romance novels. My faithful readers Courtney Taliaferro, Karen Clark, and Corinne Hegener gave me invaluable feedback.

In this memoir, I have mentioned mentors and teachers who contributed to my life, but I want to mention one more person, US Senator Fred R. Harris. It's his observation that begins the first chapter of this book. In the summer

ACKNOWLEDGMENTS

after I decided to undertake this project, I called him in New Mexico and asked him to help me with both historical facts and my memories in this writing. I also asked if he would write a blurb for the cover. He readily agreed and we had a wonderful conversation. That November I had a call from Lynda Robb telling me Fred had died. I mourn not just the passing of an old friend, but the chance to laugh over all the material you read here.

ABOUT THE AUTHOR

JANET TALIAFERRO HOLDS a BA from Southern Methodist University and an MA in Creative Studies from the University of Central Oklahoma where she received the Geoffrey Bocca Memorial Award for excellence.

This memoir chronicles her life and times, often at the center of key political and cultural events. Her novel, *A Sky for Arcadia*, was a finalist in the Oklahoma Center for the Book Award in 2001. She published another novel, two historical romances, two collections of short stories, and a chapbook of poetry. Two of her short stories were first place award winners in *The Northern Virginia Review*, and selections of her poetry have been published in small magazines.

Janet lives in Ashburn, Virginia, in the winter, and summers in Northern Wisconsin.

ABOUT BOLD STORY PRESS

BOLD STORY PRESS is a curated, woman-owned hybrid publishing company with a mission of publishing well-written stories by women. If your book is chosen for publication, our team of expert editors and designers will work with you to publish a professionally edited and designed book. Every woman has a story to tell. If you have written yours and want to explore publishing with Bold Story Press, contact us at https://boldstorypress.com.

The Bold Story Press logo, designed by Grace Arsenault, was inspired by the nom de plume, or pen name, a sad necessity at one time for female authors who wanted to publish. The woman's face hidden in the quill is the profile of Virginia Woolf, who, in addition to being an early feminist writer, founded and ran her own publishing company, Hogarth Press.

Thank you for reading my book!
If you enjoyed it, please tell a friend
and consider leaving a review on
Amazon or Goodreads—it really helps.

www.ingramcontent.com/pod-product-compliance
Lightning Source LLC
Chambersburg PA
CBHW032151080426
42735CB00008B/662